Greatest

FISHING

Joe Brooks . . . .

Greatest FISHING

Originally published in 1957

ISBN: 978-1-940001-14-2

Published by Sportsman's Vintage Press
2013

To my good friend the late Frank Bentz
of Boonsboro, Maryland.

Introduction

FROM THE STREAMS of southeastern Alaska and the Yukon territory, on down through Montana, Pennsylvania, Ontario and Maine, to the waters of the Florida Keys and the Everglades, and still further to the Isle of Pines, south of Cuba, and to the fabulous fishing waters of Tierra del Fuego and southwestern Argentina, I have followed Joe Brooks, the fishingest fisherman.

I am an envious sort of individual and even while following in Joe's footsteps I have frequently run ahead of him, trying to beat him to some particular pool because I have always had one great ambition—to catch a bigger fish some day than Joe caught that day. Finally, down on the Rio Chimehuin, in the foothills of the Andes, I did it. I took a seven pound rainbow that day, when the biggest Joe caught was about a five pound brown. But in nearly 20 years of angling with one whom I consider the greatest fly fisherman in the world, that is the only time I have ever beaten him.

A former football and baseball player, Joe brings to his fishing all the perfectionism of the true athlete and so skillful is he with his favorite fly rod that it is not unusual for other anglers to quit fishing just to watch the master angler in action.

It is not just as a fisherman, however, that Joe is great. He is best as a fishing companion, the chap who is always going out of his way to see that the other fellow's equipment is right, that he has the best flies available, and the best fishing water, and gets the first chance at the best pool. He fishes for the love of fishing. He works at it with all the fervor of an evangelist preaching religion for this is a religion with Joe. He believes that the groves are God's first temples; his communion with nature, his love of the songbirds and all of nature around him, his everlasting search for knowledge about the world of nature, make him one of the greatest outdoorsmen I have ever known.

In keeping with this feeling, Joe has always tried to pass on to others his knowledge and enthusiasm. He has taught thousands how to handle a fly and how to cast with bait and spinning rod. There are fishermen all over the country who owe their start in fishing to Joe. For instance, in his native Maryland he was one of the founders of the Brotherhood of the Jungle Cock, an organization devoted to taking youngsters fishing and teaching them the ethics of the outdoors.

Perhaps you may realize, if you have read this far, that I am a tremendous admirer of Joe Brooks. The greatest wish I could have for anyone is that someday that person might have the pleasure and experience of fishing with Joe. Barring that, he may find in this book, a worth-while and entertaining substitute. There is little that Joe has written that I haven't read and re-read. His yarns are filled with know-how, and he has the ability of taking the reader with him on the stream, the lake, or the sun-swept bonefish flats to share with him the thrill he himself derives from his favorite sport.

A Word About Lou Klewer

Writer for the Toledo Blade, Lou Klewer produces one of the most outstanding jobs of outdoor writing in America, and his lectures and pictures covering the whole outdoor field are well known in many cities throughout the country. He is current President of the Outdoor Writers Association of America, formerly having served as Chairman of the Board of Directors of the same organization for seven years; and was twice president of the Outdoor Writers of Ohio.

He was also formerly Director of the Toledo Zoological Gardens and is present President of the Toledo Zoological Society; member of the Explorers Club of New York, Toledo Naturalists Association, 30th Infantry Division Association, Marine Corps League, Arctic Institute, and numerous sportsmen's clubs and conservation organizations.

A member of the Boy Scouts of America since 1913, Mr. Klewer has been prominent in Toledo scouting, and is now a merit badge councillor, Eagle scout, holder of the Silver Beaver and William T. Hornaday gold conservation award, as well as being a member of the executive council, Toledo Boy Scouts, and member of the National Boy Scout Conservation Committee.

Foreword

IN THIS WORLD of ours, there are a few fortunate souls who earn their keep at occupations so unlike the usual concept of "work" that people remark in wonder: "And they get paid for it, too?"

Among the handful so happily employed you must certainly include a rugged, fifty-four-year-old gentleman named Joseph Brooks, of Islamorada, Florida. Joe is a professional sports fisherman—a job to make most of America's 43,000,000 other anglers drool in envy. His matchless grace and incredible accuracy in handling a fly rod, which requires the ultimate in angling skill, have led many to call him "the world's best fly fisherman." As a result, tackle manufacturers pay him well to test and use their wares, and editors ask him to write profitable, advice-filled articles and books about his angling experiences.

Brooks gathers his material by traveling some 75,000 miles a year, fishing in the most exclusive places for the most exciting fish. If the Atlantic salmon are running in Newfoundland . . . if the bonefish are roaming the tide flats off Cuba's Isle of Pines . . . if the striped bass are in at Cape Cod . . . if Argentina's giant trout are in season . . . if the arctic charr are migrating in Alaska . . . if the tarpon are on the move in Florida—Joe Brooks is likely to be there. His itinerary over the years reads like the travels of an advance scout for a tourist agency.

Twenty-odd years ago, when Joe abandoned the insurance business to become a professional angler, skeptics called him foolish to stake his fishing future exclusively on his fly rod. They claimed that only certain kinds of fish would take a fly. Brooks has proved them wrong by landing every popular fresh-water game fish and 61 species of salt-water fish on his flies. Along the way, he has set some notable records. He has caught three of the six permit—a giant relative of the pompano —ever taken with flies. He was the first ever to catch a flying fish on a fly. His 29½-pound striped bass, his 14-pound barracuda and his 18½-pound brown trout are conceded to be trophy catches for fly tackle. "Any fish that can be taken on the surface with a hook and line," says Brooks proudly, "will hit an artificial fly."

Joe also vehemently disputes the theory that fishing has declined. "The stocking program and conservation measures have meant better fishing today than we generally had 25 years ago—and it's getting even better. You know," he adds longingly, "I'd love to have this job of mine fifty years from now."

Reprinted from Collier's Magazine of April 13, 1956.

Author's Note

WHILE FLY FISHING is my first love, and my last, this book is not limited in interest to fly fishermen only. Many of the stories herein deal with spinning and plug casting as well as with deep water trolling and bait fishing. In all of them I have tried to give facts about the fishing which would be useful to any angler, regardless of his choice of tackle, and along with this practical information have tried to impart some of the romance and glamor of far places that make every fisherman yearn to seek out new and different species in distant waters.

With modern travel facilities, today these far places are not merely a dream. The airplane has brought most of them within easy reach and with every passing day the time required to reach them grows shorter. For instance, the first time I flew Pan American World Airways to Buenos Aires, the trip took 22 hours. The following year the same flight took 16 hours. Next time I go, it may well be 10 hours!

So today's traveling fisherman can go to the most remote spots even in limited vacation time. This collection of stories is prepared to help them in their choice of time, place and tackle, as well as to provide dream material for armchair anglers.

Acknowledgements

MY THANKS to the editors of *Outdoor Life, Ashaway Sportsman, The Fisherman, Field & Stream, True Fishing Annual, Fishing Waters of the World,* and *The Salt Water Sportsman* in which some portion of this material appeared.

Contents

1. Salty Grab Bag

Whether we fished beach, reef, or ocean, Bermuda kept us guessing. But—with bonefish, mackerel, wahoo, and many more—we really struck it rich.

BOBBY RAY was throwing handfuls of chum over the side of the *Iridio*, the 40-foot collection boat belonging to the Bermuda Aquarium. The chum, consisting of inchlong, hog-mouthed fry, floated along with the tide, sinking slowly in the clear blue water.

I stood on the left side of the cockpit, fly rod in hand, and Tom McNally was on the stern deck, similarly armed. We were waiting for the bottom to roll up, as it often does when you chum the Bermuda coral heads for gray snapper or any other ocean fish that might cruise by.

"Mackerel!" cried Louis Mowbray, from up forward. "Get ready. Quick."

We saw them at the extreme end of the chum, bluish-colored, torpedo-shaped fish with a multitude of spikelike finlets. These babies are built for speed. And they can't ever get a finhold on a rock and sleep, or bask on top of the water like the great, lazy ocean sunfish, for their gills are so constructed that they must keep moving or die.

Now they were into the chum, gulping up the floating *hors d'oeuvres* with lightning changes of pace. They traveled so fast that one would hit the chum unexpectedly and go into a 15-foot skid as he slammed on the brakes.

I chose one to cast a fly to, and my bucktail dropped three

feet in front of him. He made the merest swerve, snatched up
the fly, and then I was into the fastest thing on fins. The end
of the ocean was his goal. Line left the reel in a single leap and
all at once the backing was almost gone.

"Stop, fish!" I yelled. "Slow down."

Tom and Bobby looked back to see how much line I had
left.

"He's taken 650 feet already," I said. "Only 50 feet left.
Stop!" I yelled again.

And presto he came to an abrupt stop. I reeled fast.

He came my way for a second or two, then roared away
again so fast that the reel click went back into a shriek. He
started to sashay from right to left, but he was on a tack now
where I could get line back. I reeled like mad, but then let go
of the handle once more as he reversed and took off again to
the right.

He stopped sooner this time, and then I kept at him, beginning to pull him my way. In he came, foot by foot. Then he
pawed the water hard and away he went, taking 100 feet of
line before he slowed. But when he stopped this time, I kept
him coming, and when he was close to the boat I saw the long
handled net go out. I raised the rod tip and dragged that spent
fish into the net.

Bobby lifted him aboard. He weighed 7¾ pounds.

"What a fish!" I gasped.

"It's the same fish they call false albacore or little tuna," said
Louie, who's Curator of the Bermuda Aquarium. "Mostly he's
taken on trolling gear."

"He's a whiz-bang on a fly rod." I commented. "Where are
the others?"

"Gone," said Bobby. "These fish are fast travellers. They
probably picked up the scent of our chum a quarter of a mile
away and followed it in. Now they've gone somewhere else."

Five minutes after the mackerel fight subsided, the snappers
down below decided that all was clear. Then it really did look
as if the bottom were rolling up, as a school of snappers showed,

at first indistinct, then clearer as it broke the surface, feeding fast and without caution. A dark line extending backwards a couple of inches over each eye of the fish grew blacker and blacker, registering their excitement over the feast as a thermometer registers fever.

"Wait till those lines are really black," said Louie, "then cast. But be sure to let the fly float free. Don't move it at all. The snappers want it dead, like chum."

I dropped the same inch-long white bucktail I'd used for the mackerel and watched it float slowly along.

A four-pound snapper raced for it but turned away at the last second. I was so sure he had it that I struck and my line flew high in the air.

I dropped the fly again. A snapper hit it right off and was cellar-bound. He didn't stop until he'd wrapped my leader around a rock and cut me off.

The commotion scared the other fish and they all headed down. But Bobby tossed out another handful of chum and in a few minutes they were topside again and in there pitching, their black lines throbbing with greed.

I heard Tom shout as he was into one. His snapper dived, then levelled off, halfway down and darted away for 100 feet. Soon it turned, got sideways to the boat, and pulled a healthy bend into Tom's rod. But Tom didn't back up, and as the pressure told, the fish came slowly up and into the net.

"Not an ounce over three pounds," said Tom. "And I thought he was seven or eight."

The gray or mangrove snapper is one of the strongest fish of the ocean. So far as is known, a 16-pounder is the largest ever taken on fly or spinning tackle. They have the strength to go into a terrific power dive and cut you off on the rocks. And besides brawn they have brains. They have eyes like an eagle, and their ability to spot a phony is one of the reasons they're dubbed sea lawyers.

"Did you ever notice that fish in the live well?" Louie asked us. "Of all the fish we put in there, when we're collecting for the aquarium, only the snappers try to escape. They stick their heads above the water, looking for a way out."

"They're smart, all right," we all agreed.

"If they weren't such gluttons, they'd never get caught," said Louie.

"Do any other fish have that feeding line?" I asked.

"Quite a few," he answered. "Amberjacks, bonito, and in a different way the wahoos and marlin, which have vertical bars that show more plainly when they're feeding."

This Bermuda fishing was like dipping into a salty grab bag. You never knew what might come out. It might be a five-pound yellowtail, a 10-pound bonito, or a great amberfish. Or it might be a school of ocean robins (related to the jacks), or some specimen never before recorded by icthyologists. This was the middle of June. I wondered how long this kind of fishing could hold up.

As if reading my mind, Brose Gosling spoke. "April to the end of October is when we get the biggest variety," he said. "But you can catch something here all year."

On our way in that day we stopped to fish a deep coral head that we'd picked up with the echo finder. Again we tossed chum overboard and cast into it. A large, whitish fish came slowly up and took my fly. I struck, but too late. That fish had discovered something wrong and spit the fly right out. More chum brought him up once more, this time with a friend. One of them took the fly and again I struck and missed.

Next time he showed I outfoxed him. As soon as he was within half an inch of the bucktail, I struck and caught him with the fly in his mouth. Then he turned it on. He was a terrific fighter for a two-pounder.

"That's a triggerfish," said Louis, when at last I led it into the net. "Pirates of the sea, they are. During the war when sailors were shipwrecked and floating on rafts, a triggerfish would ease up to the raft and take a nip out of a leg or arm dangling in the water."

"They don't stop at a nip, either," said Bobby.

Author and Captain Roy Taylor admire the 14 pound barracuda that Brooks took on 10 pound monofilament line.

"No," agreed Louis. "They're like the piranha. They'd take all of your flesh off you, bite by bite, if you fell into a school of them."

Bermuda is a 22-mile strip of islands shaped like a fishhook, as if to point out that there's some wonderful fishing around the islands which in the past have owed their fame mostly to

honeymooners. Even the beautiful pink beaches have their share
of unique fishing, notably the flashy gaff-topsail pompano that
swim within easy reach of a cast lure.

As I stepped off the Pan American plane on my first trip to
Bermuda, Jimmy Williams met me with a loaf of bread tucked
under one arm.

"No time to waste," he said. "We'll leave your luggage here
till later and go right out to the beach."

"Dry bread for lunch at a beach party?" I asked.

Jimmy grinned. "This bread is for the pompano," he explained. "For chum. You throw bits of bread out and they start
feeding on it, then you bait your hook with another bit, and
cast."

Maybe they'll hit a fly, I suggested.

They did, and we also caught pompano on small fly rod size
spoons. First they hit well inshore. Then as they grew cautious
and moved further out, we moved out too, until we were
shoulder-deep in the water, beyond the crash of the breakers.

Those fish reached up to four pounds, and any gaff-topsail
pompano over a pound will give you a scrappy fight on either
fly or spinning tackle.

That day we used bread. On later occasions we chummed
with hog-mouthed fry and took two bonefish, a four-pound
bonito, and some pompano.

Some of the biggest bonefish in the world have been taken
from Bermuda's inshore waters, and at one time three world
records were posted for the island. One of them, a 14-pounder
caught in Shelley Bay by Dr. H. R. Becker of York, Pa., still
holds lead position in the 20-pound line-test class of the International Game Fish Association.

It's a tough job to take most Bermuda fish on straight away
casting without use of chum, because the water is so clear. But
the bonefish is one which inshore anglers can reach by wading
or by skiff. And Bermuda bonefish present a special challenge.
They seem particularly strong, they're found in deeper, clearer
water than most other places—hence are more difficult to spot

Eugene Meyer, of Bermuda, Captain of the British Empire Tuna Team in 1956, holds up the 20 pound wahoo he landed on 10 pound line.

and cast to before they see you and swim away—and there's always a chance of a record fish.

On a trip to Whale Harbor with Pete Perinchief and George Morris, I noticed that they were constantly making quick, jerky movements with their heads as they waded along, so as to get a better view through the water with their Polaroid glasses.

Suddenly Pete stopped and stood there, snapping his head from side to side. "Shadows," he reported.

"Are you nuts?" asked George. "There can't be; there isn't a cloud in the sky."

"Bonefish shadows," said Pete.

And then I remembered. Pete and I had fished here a few years ago on a day when we couldn't spot the fish but could see their shadows against the sandy bottom. Even while I was remembering, Pete made his cast and was into a fish.

A second later George yelled "There's another." And he was fast to a speedster that was on his way to Cuba. George knew it was useless to try to stop that run.

"He'll clean me," he said. "He's gone 200 yards already."

But that big salt water reel had plenty of line. George got the bonefish coming back our way, though he fought all the way in and then went off again on a 150-foot run before George finally towed him in for keeps.

"Ten pounds," he said, as he put him back. "What a runner."

Besides bonefish, gaff-topsail pompano and gray snapper, anglers fishing the beaches, shallow bays and coral heads of Bermuda can take barracuda, gwelly, chub, and occasionally a yellowtail or a prowling bonito. Farther out, over 25 fathoms, they can connect with yellowtails, bonito, mackerel (false albacore), ocean robins, and many other surface cruising fish. Also, deep-sea charter boats troll for Allison tuna, Bermuda tuna, dolphin, wahoo, white marlin, blue marlin, and mako. Occasional visitors to Bermuda waters are tarpon, bluefish, horse-eye jacks, jack crevalle, and blue-fin tuna.

But one of the greatest thrills of deep-water fishing is that you may come up with just about anything. Louis Mowbray has done many kinds of fishing in his search, but one of the most interesting is his "deep-line" work at night.

"That's when the deep dwellers come to or near the top," he explained. "They don't like the light rays and so only move up when it's dark."

By deep-line fishing, after dark, he's collected the terrible-tempered tapioca or oilfish and the rare Bermuda ocean catfish. He's landed great tuna and albacore at night, and just recently made one of the great icthyological finds of the century when he caught a lancet fish. Only three of these creatures are known to have been caught on hook and line, and none of them reached scientific hands, so all previous information about them came from specimens washed ashore in a decomposed state.

The lancet is an elongated, scaleless, and almost boneless fish with a high, sail-like dorsal fin. Mowbray's specimen was 41 inches long, four inches wide. It took a garfish bait at 30 fathoms

With things like this to intrigue the curious, more and more anglers are sure to go deep trolling and drifting in Bermuda waters, and I for one would like to be in on it when some new, strange and terrible-looking monster comes protestingly up from the depths.

One of my own strangest catches there, to date, has been a flying fish. That day the water was so rough that we couldn't see if any fish were coming to our chum line.

"I'll fix that," said Louie, who has a remedy for every piscatorial ailment.

He ducked into the cabin for a small bottle of dark-colored liquid which he started sprinkling overboard. The drops spread quickly and a film began to cover the water downtide from us.

"Shark oil," said Louie. "It calms rough seas. It's a weather gauge, too. If bad weather is coming, the fluid will cloud up."

Through the water, now flattened and cleared by the shark oil, we could see flying fish, close to the boat.

I got a hook—baited with fry—out there fast, and saw one of those little seagoing butterflies take. We landed several that day and found that they're just about the tastiest morsel in the ocean.

Next day we went for Bermuda chub.

"I'll bet you can't land one over four pounds on either fly or spinning gear," said Louie on the way out to the reef. "They'll dive to the bottom and cut you off on a rock."

"They get as heavy as 18 pounds," added Pete Perinchief. "But even on heavy tackle the average landed is four pounds."

That day we were chumming with chunks of lobster.

"You'd better bait with lobster, too," suggested Louie. "They hit bait better than flies or lures."

But I wanted to try my own choice of lures. I started with a fly, and the chunky fish hit that fine, but they were hard to

Fishing the beaches at Bermuda for gaff-topsail pompano. With miles of such water, and lots of pompano, whole families get in on the fun.

hook. Finally I managed to hook two but lost both of them in a hurry.

I changed to spinning gear and lost two more. They went down under some rocks and cut me off, just as Louie had said. Seeing the writing on the wall, I picked up a big trolling outfit with 20-pound-test line and finally brought in a two-pounder. Then I fought it out with a 2½-pounder that acted more like a whale.

The third one to hit was a monster who all but tore the rod from my hands. He ripped line from the reel in spite of the heavy drag.

"You may only have seen them up to 18 pounds," I told Pete. "But I'll bet this one's over 20."

When I finally got him in, he weighed 4½ pounds. I took my hat off to that chub.

All the while we had been fishing, Capt. Roy Taylor had been in touch with other charter boats around Bermuda. We'd hear him give the call letters of his boat, the *Wally III*, then, when some other boat came in, he'd ask:

"How's fishing?"

Capt. Lewis Martin of the *Sea Wolf* reported a 128-pound white marlin just landed. Capt. Charlie Christianson chimed in to tell us there were wahoo in his neighbourhood.

"Better get over here," he advised. "There are some good. ones."

We wasted no time heading that way. The record for wahoo in Bermuda waters is 110 pounds, while the average taken there ranges from 35 to 45 pounds.

The wahoo probably got his name from the excited shout of the first angler who ever hooked one. He's a streamlined, vertical-barred powerhouse that makes fanatics out of those who connect with him. I've met anglers who will go for no other fish, period. And the wahoo is the fish most often named by charter-boat captains who have told me their favorite catch.

"That bait is a tantalizing thing," I thought, as I sat in the fighting chair, watching the one-pound garfish bait dance along the surface. It jumped from wave to wave. Once it disappeared and I sat bolt upright, ready and hopeful. But it reappeared, skipping along, throwing up splashes of water.

The sun was bright, the waves were a couple of feet high, providing just the right action and oxygen, at the surface, for a cruising wahoo.

My eyes dropped and I shook my head. This was the way many a guy had lost a good fish. I shook my head again and looked at the bait. Nothing back of it, and only the waves and the deep blue of the ocean around it.

I glanced up at the outrigger. The 10-pound-test line was fast in the clothespin up there. The captain had advised a heavier line, but I wanted to go light.

"This could go on all day," I thought to myself, as we churned along. My head drooped again. For how long, I don't know.

"Fish!" shouted Roy Taylor. "Fish! Fish! Wahoo! Back of your bait!"

My eyes popped open a foot and I saw the brown shape right under the bait. I took one quick look at the outrigger, to see that everythig was O.K. up there, then yanked my eyes back to the skipping bait just in time to see it taken.

Barrels of water flew upward and again I looked to the outrigger. This time the line came out of the clothespin and was suddenly tight between the fish and my rod. I struck hard twice. Then, as I felt that bozo, I braced myself and watched one of angling's greatest sights—a wahoo churning the ocean into lines of bursting bubbles as he surged on top, getting up speed with every swipe of his crescent-shaped tail. This fish was faster than thought. His surges covered 50 feet, and then he slipped into high and struck a pace that made those surges seem like pygmy efforts. He charged across the ocean just under the surface for 1,000 feet.

Then the line went slack, and every drop of blood in my veins ran to my feet. I'd wanted that fish so badly.

"He's not off," the captain observed. "He's reversed, that's all. He just showed out there."

The line came tight again, and I felt him. I tightened the drag and began to pump him. He was slower now, tired after that terrific burst of speed. Soon we could see his outline lying broadside to the boat. Slowly I worked him in.

"A 40-pounder," said Captain Roy. "A nice fish."

Then, "Shark! Shark!"

The wahoo saw the shark at the same moment we did. He accelerated even faster than he had the first time. But we knew it couldn't last. The fish was too tired, and pulling against the drag of the reel didn't help any.

I looked at Roy, then pointed the big rod right at the wahoo. I felt the 10-pound-test monofilament line come up in the water, saw it straighten out, and then heard the crack of the line as it parted.

"I couldn't sit here and watch that shark get him," I said.

"You and me both," said Roy. "I'd have done the same thing."

Out there we saw the shark give up the chase. He turned and came back toward us, as if he'd like to get even with us for letting his meal get away. Then, as he got closer, he sank from view.

We were thinking just as nasty things about him. That was a fish we had wanted. But after a while we began to feel better. That wahoo would live to fight another battle, to give some other angler, or maybe even me, another thrill, the great feel of being tied to a seagoing comet.

2. Bonefish Bonanza

**A voyage of discovery to the Isle of Pines, Cuba—
Robert Louis Stevenson's "Treasure Island."**

"BONEFISH," I said. "Bonefish."

I imitated the swishing noise of a jet plane going by, then waggled my fingers, trying to make like a bonefish tailing.

"No comprendo," Obilio, the taxi driver, said.

"Like a comet! Agua! Bubbles!" chimed in Vic, and he and Jean joined me in producing a hullabaloo of noises and hand wiggles designed to suggest a bonefish taking off across a flat.

"Momento!" exclaimed Obilio as he dove into the pocket of his shirt, produced a stubby pencil, and then with deft fingers lifted the envelope containing my plane ticket from my own pocket and handed the two to me.

No further words were necessary. Quickly I drew a rough sketch of a bonefish and shoved it in front of Obilio.

"Ah! Ah-ha!" he exclaimed in a tone of great discovery. "Macabi! Si, si! Macabi!" He spread his arms to embrace the whole island in a magnanimous gesture. "Mucho macabi!"

Vic Barothy, well-known Florida Keys resort operator, Jean Crooks, veteran Miami fly caster, and I had just landed in the land of the Latins, flying in from Key West to Havana and then hopping southward again via Aerovias "Q" to Cuba's picturesque little Isle of Pines, believed by many to be the inspiration for Stevenson's "Treasure Island."

15

We had been hearing rumors about great numbers of bone-fish in Cuban waters and we wanted to check these reports.

Obilio had met us at the airport, as if by appointment, gravely handing us a card which stated "English spoken." And without further ado he escorted us to his taxi cab which stood waiting on the very doorstep of the airport office.

Obilio's taxi, a Model A Ford, painted a bright yellow, was quickly christened "The Yellow Peril," but it was the best available method of getting around. From our headquarters at the Isle of Pines Hotel, at Neuva Gerona, we went with Obilio to many parts of the island during our stay and discovered beaches where probably no one but ourselves had ever fished.

Our first trip was to the west coast of the island, a 25-mile ride through rolling country, with views of the 1,500-foot mountains which are the outstanding scenic feature. Along the roads grew the tallest Royal Palms I have ever seen. In addition there was stand after stand of bottle palms, from the swollen midsection of which dugout canoes were often made. All the way across to our fishing grounds we saw paired quail and white crowned pigeons and doves galore.

At last we came out on a long, sandy bay that looked plenty fishy. The three of us hit the beach simultaneously, almost before the Yellow Peril had settled its shakes. We broke all records getting our fly tackle together. Vic headed up the beach to the right, I hustled down to the left, and Jean went straight out from where we had stopped. Before I had gone a hundred feet I heard Jean shout. I turned and saw his rod bent almost double. Probably the first Isle of Pines bonefish ever to swat a fly was racing for the deep.

"Macabi!" shouted Jean.

"Macabi!" I yelled back.

And from far down the beach, like an echo, we heard Vic's cry, "Macabi!"

On the running board of the Yellow Peril, Obilio stood with one hand fondly placed on the yellow hood, and the other, palm up, as if conferring a blessing.

An Isle of Pines bonefish is giving the angler a busy time.

"Ha!" he said. "Macabi! Mucho, mucho macabi!"

In the course of my fishing days I've seen lots of bonefish. On the Florida Keys I've seen a thousand of them on one bank at one time. Schools of a hundred are not an every day sight, but certainly not unusual. That one day on the Isle of Pines, however, I saw more bonefish than I had ever seen in a week's time before. They were everywhere. Singles, doubles, quartettes, schools of twenty, fifty, a hundred and more went by in formation. One great mass of them that passed me must have held 500 fish in its ranks.

Where I had started to fish, the bottom was sandy and you

could see a fish for a long way. The sun was at my back and the first thing that caught my eye was a huge, shadowy blotch on the bottom. It seemed to be moving slowly my way and for a moment I thought that it must be a manatee or a great manta ray. I adjusted my Polaroid glasses and looked again. And then I realized that it was a tremendous school of bonefish. So I didn't take to the woods and climb the nearest tree. Instead I dropped a fly right in front of the oncoming horde.

A dozen fish saw that fly and all of them wanted it. They bumped into each other going for it. I struck as I felt one connect, and I was fast to my first Cuban macabi.

That Spanish version of the fish that makes like a comet acted as if he didn't know he was hooked. He stayed right with the school and the school kept coming straight at me.

I stood there frozen for a minute. Then I came to, tightened up enough to let him know that everything was not as serene as he seemed to think. The feel of that hook turned him wild. He started off for the deep, striking other fish in the school, spreading panic as he went, until at last the whole kit and kaboodle of them was racing for the deep, throwing water high and charging across that flat like a herd of wild horses.

I managed to extract my fish from that surging, sea-going school and finally brought him in. He looked to weigh about four pounds as I took the hook out of the corner of his mouth and put him back in the water.

As I turned and looked down the flat again, I spotted more fish coming, several tails already flashing in the sun. Then, off by itself I saw a big, dark shape, a hundred feet away, slowly moving in my direction. It looked longer than a bonefish should, but at that distance I couldn't be sure. I strained my eyes in their sockets and edged a couple of steps closer. The fish turned broadside and I was pretty sure it was a permit. But suddenly he swam my way, nosing the bottom and sending up little puffs of mud as he searched for prey in the sand and grass.

"Smokin'!" I said aloud. "A-smokin' and a-puffin'—not a permit, but a really big bonefish! Maybe the biggest macabi on the whole Isle of Pines, and I'm the guy that's going to trade punches with him."

But then I lost him again and though I popped my eyes out, I couldn't locate him. And just as I was about ready to give up and forget him, that macabi stood on his head twenty feet in front of me, did a hula with his caudal and like to scared me out of my boots. Somehow I got a fly in front of him, saw him charge. I set the hook and held the rod high as he steamed out of there, heading for the rim of keys five miles off shore. After about 200 feet he broke his headlong sprint and slanted down the shoreline as if to dash himself to pieces on the rocks. But he didn't do that. Instead, he cut the 8-pound test tippet on something sharp and the slack line let my rod snap back into shape.

"Hasta la vista!" I shouted after him, and I was very sincere in that parting wish.

The next day we left from the Jucaro River in a skiff powered by an outboard which we had toted all the way from Key West. We went two miles down-stream until we came to the ocean. Here, on the east side of the island we found somewhat deeper water, but at high tide the fish seemed to be in and we could spot them as they cruised across sandy patches.

When the tide ebbed, we decided to drop Jean on a half mile stretch of sandy shoreline while Vic and I went farther down the beach to similar spots. At my appointed place, the sand reached out 150 feet from the shore and the water deepened gradually until it was about knee deep at the outside edge of the bar.

I slipped into ankle-depth water and looked for tailers. And it didn't take long to spot a regular procession of them, going in a circle, tails a-wagging, feeding avidly. I had on a small white bucktail, tied on a number 2 hook. On the whole, these macabi seemed small and having found that they were hitting short on the longer streamers, I turned to the smallest fly I had. I cast to the tailers only forty feet away and so intent were they that I pulled my fly back without them seeing it. My next

An Isle of Pines bonefish is landed and released.

cast dropped in the middle of the circle and this time they all seemed to see it at once. Out of the wild scramble, one got there first and gobbled it up entirely. I set the hook and watched the sand fly as the whole school followed the hooked fish.

He headed right down the middle of the sandy patch, flushing bonefish right and left, then doubled back a way, slashed off toward the deep, and dropped the hook. By the time I reached the end of that sandy patch, I had landed and released six bonefish and lost five. A total of eleven fish hooked in a half mile stretch and in an hour of fishing is worth going a long way for. And it is not unusual on the Isle of Pines.

As I neared the end of my sandy spot I noticed Vic standing off a point ahead of me so I scrambled ashore and walked on down. He was fighting a fish, and released it as I watched him.

"It's been like this ever since I got here," he shouted at me. "I just stand here on this spot and wait for them to come to me. Boy, what fishing!"

That afternoon was like all the rest of the trip. Bonefish were everywhere and we had strikes and fights most of the time. The third day was the same. Once again we fished out of the Jucaro, but this time we headed north when we reached the ocean, and as before we left the boat at strategic points, fished out a stretch of beach then gathered together at lunch time to swap experiences. When we figured it out, we found that the first day the three of us had landed 31 bonefish up to six pounds and had lost almost as many. The second day we had almost matched that and the third was just as good.

It was almost dark when we headed into the dock that third day, but when we saw tarpon rolling on the other side of the river, we couldn't resist them. Vic steered that way and cut the motors. Jean started casting. He was using only an 8-pound-test leader and those rolling silver kings, called "sabalo" here, looked to be hundred pound fish, but even so, when one rolled up right in front of the boat, Jean dropped his fly practically in its mouth. It hit, and came roaring up, 35 pounds of silver dynamite, and for half an hour fought like mad. Then it tired and Jean brought the tarpon to boat and Vic grasped the leader and took the fly out.

We watched the tarpon swim away.

"Sabalo too!" mused Jean, running his fingers along the leader where the tarpon's gill covers had roughed it. "Sabalo and macabi both .`. .!"

As we headed in, we heard a soft, inquisitive chattering coming out of the dusk. We looked up and sweeping across the mangroves came a flight of tree ducks. They flew off into the darkness across the river, their piping and whistling fading off to a whisper. Night had fallen and it was good to be alive under Cuban stars.

When we pulled up to the dock, Obilio was waiting.

"Macabi?" he asked anxiously.

"Macabi," we nodded. "Mucho, mucho macabi!"

3. Next Time We'll Leave The Ladies Home

As a result of the exploratory trip described in BONEFISH BONANZA, Vic Barothy bought land and developed a fishing camp on the Jucaro River. Three years later, Jean Crooks and I went back, taking our wives along. We joined the Barothys in further exploration, going to the outer Keys this time, some miles from the Isle of Pines.

NOT ALL WIVES are willing fishing widows, especially when plans are being made for an extra-good trip like this one, to fish the remote keys to the eastward of the Isle of Pines, Cuba. Jean Crooks, Vic Barothy and I were deep in discussion of the reports we'd heard of the unfished waters down there, of great hordes of bonefish, huge permit, acres of tarpon.

"Sounds good to me," spoke up Jean's wife, Virginia. "When do we go?"

We all looked up, startled. This was "men only."

"If bonefish are that thick . . ." I heard Mary say.

"And hundreds of tarpon . . ." Betty chimed in. "Maybe we poor females have a chance to catch a fish for a change."

That was how the six of us happened to be headed out from the Isle of Pines on Vic's houseboat, the Jucaro, on a warm day last January. We were towing three skiffs and were headed for Cayo del Rosario, sixty miles away.

All day we ran past keys covered with mangroves, palm

23

trees, and mahogany trees that looked big and black against the bright blue skies. We saw little blue herons, cormorants, man o'war birds, American egrets, black-crowned night herons, and white ibis. Occasionally, in the distance, we spotted a "lobster boat" anchored with sail up while the crew, two to a skiff, worked their bully nets in ten feet of water, grappling and grabbing the spiny crawfish, called langosta in Cuban waters.

We cruised by Cayo Bocas de Alonza, Cayo Campos (where the charts show fresh-water wells), and Cayo Aguardientes—romantic names for wild and strange-looking islands. We had been told that as far as rod-and-reel fishing was concerned, this was all virgin water, and we wanted to stop and fish. We did make casts as we slowed to go through the narrow channels between the islands but the water was so fishy looking that we knew that if we anchored and took to skiffs we would never be able to tear ourselves away and go on. And from what we had heard about Rosario, that was the ultimate. It was better than anyplace. So we went on, counting the cays, bead by bead, praying for what had been promised at Rosario.

Just before sunset we raised the island, working cautiously between the shallow shore and the jagged black teeth of a dry shingle reef that reared up off to our right, out of the ocean fathoms. We eased over a bottom that was alternately brilliant green and dark purple and brown, where heads of rocks and grasses showed. We gave those rocks a wide berth, because the up-jutting coral formations could tear the beams out of a boat. And at last Lloyd Garcia, the Cuban member of our party, dropped anchor right on the spot he had previously marked on our charts as headquarters for the next few days.

Leaving the women on board to prepare a late supper, the rest of us went fishing. Jean and I ran down the channel a short distance and anchored, while Vic and Lloyd went on past us a couple of hundred feet. On Jean's first cast, a 15-pound tarpon bolted his bug, and when the tarpon felt the hook he bounced four feet out of the water, did a jack-knife, and splashed back in again. He looked golden against the glow

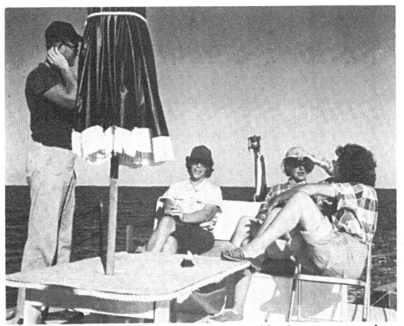

On the way out to the fishing grounds, the girls plot up a storm, leave Jean Crooks wondering about these fishing wives!

of the reddening sky. Then I had a hit, too, and this time both fish came out together, went back in, and shot off abreast like a team of pacers. Our reels sang high as those silvery thunderbolts took off. It was 15 minutes before we landed them. And although we fished until 11 p.m., and must have jumped 50 tarpon apiece, we didn't boat another. But we felt all right about it. What matter if we released them by hand at the boat's edge or by accident out there in the darkness a few hundred feet. With tarpon, the jump is the thing, and those tarpon jumped the way they were supposed to jump.

When we returned to the houseboat, the women greeted us coldly.

"That sounded like fun," they said. "From now on, we go, too."

"This is your party," we agreed. "From now on, we'll let you ladies do all the fishing you want."

We didn't expect them to take us literally.

As we ate our supper, Lloyd told us more about Rosario.

"Lots of commercial fishermen camp here overnight, sometimes for several days," he said. "They get tired of staying on their 14-foot boats with nothing to do but look in the live wells at the langosta."

"What's on the island?" we wanted to know. "Any game?"

"Just pigeons and small iguana," he said. "And lots of queen conchs along the shore. Fishermen get them for food and for bait, too. Then there's an old fresh-water well. And there are the graves."

"What graves?" asked Betty.

"Fifty years ago a fishing boat piled up on the reef out there," said Lloyd. "Five men drowned. Somebody buried them over there on the island. Each grave is marked with a cross made of driftwood and wreaths made from palm leaves. And every once in a while, fresh mangrove blossoms. Nobody knows who does that," Lloyd shrugged. "Maybe some fishermen. Maybe la dama en negra."

"Lady in black?" asked Mary. "Who is she?"

"Nobody knows," said Lloyd, looking out into the darkness. "She comes at night, but she has been seen leaving the graves in the early morning, walking down the beach. No one has seen the boat, no one knows where she goes. But there will be new crosses there and fresh flowers and wreaths. They say she is old now, and bent," he went on. "Walks with a cane."

"Maybe she's the wife of one of those men. Fifty years!" I shook my head. "That's a long time to tend a grave."

Next morning we all made a bee-line for the graves. There they were, five lonely burial plots, each marked with a pile of coral rock and queen conch shells. At the top end of one there was a big piece of brain coral, and each had its little driftwood cross hung with dried wreaths of mangrove blossoms. We doffed our hats. I thought to myself that maybe those guys were running a handline along the drop-off of heaven now and were into a nice school of mackerel. Maybe they'd stop their fishing awhile to look down at their graves at Rosario, at the steady procession of land crabs, the schools of tailing bonefish, the flashy progress of a feeding permit. Up there where fish are fat, plentiful and sporty, they wouldn't begrudge us our try at their old waters around Rosario.

Afterwards, Mary and I ran our skiff down to the end of the island. There I cut the motor and started poling. The water was as clear as a newly washed window. Right away we found some tarpon, lazing in a round, sandy hole. They lay there crisscrossed, at different levels; some were tail to tail, others nose to nose. Only one of them moved, a 20-pounder rolling on the back edge of the school.

"Those tarpon are asleep," I said. "Put on a popping bug, and we'll wake them up."

Marys' first cast hit right over a dozen sleeping fish. She popped the bug hard. One fish switched his caudal fin and moved forward a foot. That was all.

But the second pop did it. All came topside fast. One of them got there ahead of the others. He opened his big mouth, and the bug dropped in. Mary struck too soon, and the popper flew high in the air. But she had it back on the surface before I could say, "Hey!"

This time a 30-pounder gobbled it, went deep, careened across the bottom, scattering tarpon like wildfire, and then zoomed up, crashing through the surface and out into the sunshine. He did a rumba across the top on his tail, sloshed back in, and ran smack into another tarpon. Both fish stopped dead for a split-second, then went their separate ways. Neither one came back. The bug popped to the surface, and Mary reeled it in, talking all the while about how those two 50-pound fish rammed each other, and the one had knocked the bug right out of the mouth of the hooked fish.

"It was a heck of a thing to do," I agreed, upstaking. "Let's find some more fish."

When we got back to the houseboat for lunch, Jean and Virginia were already there.

"What luck?" I asked Jean.

"I spent the morning catching snappers," he said sourly.

We looked over the bucket of snappers, one of the best "eating fish" on the menu.

"Well, what are you looking so glum about?" we asked. "Don't you like to catch snappers, especially nice big ones like those?"

"Sure," he said. "Sure, I like to catch snappers. But not when I'm casting to the biggest permit you ever saw."

It seemed that for half an hour he and Virginia had trailed a big permit that was moving down the beach—feeding, swimming, tailing unconcernedly. And every time they would get within casting distance, and Jean would toss a fly in front of that big fish, a snapper would grab his lure. By the time he got rid of the snapper and was ready to cast again, the permit would be far down the shore, and he would have to pole fast to catch up.

"Snappers were everywhere," he grumbled. "Under rocks where they're supposed to be, and on the sand bars where they have no right to be. They were even going by in big schools, and every one of them was hungry. I'm sick and tired of snappers. By the time I had landed the twelfth, that big permit had begun to suspect something was wrong, and he got out of there. I never did get a real good cast to him."

"Well, you have our sympathy," laughed Vic. "And those snappers are just right for supper."

On the charts, the dry-shingle reef that formed a barrier for the whole length of the island was shown as rising out of 200 fathoms of ocean, but on our side the depth was only from two to 15 feet. As we ran out to explore, we could see white-capped breakers rolling up against the outer side. Beneath us the water was smooth and clear, and we could look down to rocky caverns where snappers and groupers just had to be hiding.

Mary made the first cast into five feet of emerald-tinted water, and a dozen fish came roaring out of those caverns, all bent for that surface fooler. Then from underneath, rising majestically, came a great Cuban snapper that must have weighed 25 pounds. The small fry saw him the same moment we did, apparently, and flew that popper fast. With regal calmness, the great snapper floated up, opened its mouth, and the bug went down like a chip over the lip of Niagara. I looked at Mary and her eyes were out on sticks. She never did set the hook. She was frozen as she watched that beast turn and start down. He went home without even knowing he was hooked, neatly slicing the leader in two on a sharp rock and leaving us to wonder how long it would take him to digest that tenite bug. After the way he had swooshed it gulletwards, we knew it was well down inside.

While we were re-rigging, we heard a yelp from one of the other boats. Betty had hooked something on her spinning gear. She was pulling and hauling and treating that outfit like no light tackle should be treated, but she couldn't move whatever it was down under the boat.

"Must be a big grouper," Vic called to us. "She can't budge him."

He turned the motor on, backed off and made a complete circle around the rocks into which they had been casting. We let our boat drift closer to watch the fun.

"He's coming up!" yelled Betty, and she began to pump. She pumped and pumped, and at last we could see the big dark shape as she worked it closer to the skiff.

Vic slipped the net under the fish and boated him and then Betty proudly held it up. It was an eight-pound "gag," a big grouper and an excellent catch for the distaff side.

No sooner had she dropped her lure in again when she was fast to something else.

"I've got another!" she cried, and then her voice fell. "Must be little."

"Acts like grass," said Vic. "It's not pulling. Reel 'er in."

Her lure came in dragging a foot length of leader and a yellow plug behind it.

Lloyd's mouth fell open. "We lost that plug two weeks ago

Houseboat heading out the Jucaro River for remote keys.

at Cayo Campos," he said in an awed tone. "Hazen Jones had a strike, and the fish broke the line, took plug and all. It must be the same one, because no one else has fished out here."

"These Cuban fish are traveling senors," said Vic. "It's ten miles from here to Campos."

"Maybe it'll bring me luck," said Betty. "I'm going to fish with it."

Vic and I both gave her a disgusted look, because it seemed to us that the women in this party were covered with luck. But he tied the lure on for her in place of her former one.

She cast a couple of times and then had a slashing strike.

"A small 'cuda," she cried, as she reeled it in.

"That's a funny looking 'cuda, isn't it, Joe?" said Vic, holding it up.

"That's a sennett!" I exclaimed. "It's a member of the 'cuda family, all right. Common in Bermuda and the Bahamas, but very rare here."

Betty was all self-satisfied smiles, while Vic and I felt grimmer than ever. Not satisfied with catching the most and the biggest fish, these women were going after the rare ones, too. We wondered what she would produce next.

But the next cast she hooked a big snapper, and this was a crafty one. Down he went, sawed the line across a rock, and was gone. We figured from the way he got out of there, that this very lure he took with him would probably turn up next in the Caymen Islands, a hundred miles to the eastward.

As we ran back to the Jucaro just at dusk, we came on Jean and Virginia anchored in a channel. Virginia stood up to exhibit her first tarpon on spinning tackle, a beautiful 13-pounder.

Later, as we congratulated her, she grinned widely. "I don't know which I'm proudest of, the tarpon or the two bonefish."

"What two bonefish?" we asked.

"While you were all fishing the reefs this morning," said Jean, "I took Virginia over on the flats to give her a lesson in fly casting. She caught two bonefish."

That night after dinner, talk got around to permit. Permit had been one of the reasons we wanted to explore this water. We liked bonefish and tarpon and big snapper, too, but permit, that spooky will-o'-the-wisp of the salty flats—that was the fish we really wanted.

We talked about the various baits they would hit and dug into our lure boxes trying to match up artificials that looked like their favorite foods. I picked out an inch-long white bucktail with grizzly hackle, tied on a No. 2 hook.

"That's a lot like a small worm I've seen in the coral rock," I said "A worm about an inch long, with grayish white body blotched with black. I found one in the stomach of a permit once, too."

Lloyd shook his head dubiously. "I never heard of them taking anything but bait," he said. "But you can try. Maybe we should go around to the other side of the island. Over there

vou'll find smaller ones. Here you're liable to get a strike
from one that goes maybe 80 pounds."

We all grinned at each other. "We won't mind," we assured
him.

The next day was a big one on the flats around Rosario.
Every one of us chalked up bonefish, one after the other. We
had them on in pairs and triplets, the skiffs almost within casting distance of each other, the hooked fish almost crossing
each other in their anxiety to get out of there. They were in
there like mice, and just as hungry. By lunch time, we were
all bonefish-happy, our ears buzzing with the zing of the reels
as those Cuban macabi made like comets.

As we pulled away from the Jucaro after lunch, I dug into
my pocket and pulled out my special permit fly. I spit on it
for luck.

"After you've caught one·more bonefish," I warned Mary,
"I'm going to tie on this fly, and it's going to be my turn to
fish. And we're going to look for permit."

But Mary never did catch that next bonefish. Because it
wasn't ten minutes later that we both saw that big, black,
sickle-shaped tail poke out of the water a hundred feet down
the shore.

"Permit!" we both yelled.

Gallantry had no place then.

"One side, women," I muttered, snatching the fly rod out
of Mary's hand and shoving the poling pole at her. "Get me
into casting range."

I fumbled frantically in my pocket for my special permit
fly and tied it on the end of the leader. By that time the permit
was tailing 65 feet away. I got the line in the air, cast, and
watched the fly fall a foot in front of him. I began the retrieve. His tail disappeared. There was mud out there where
he had been rooting, but I couldn't see the fish. Where was he?
My eyes strained in their sockets. Then there he was, right
back of the fly, going for it with his back almost out of water.
I held my breath. He had it, quick, and as I rammed home the

hook, he turned and headed for the dry shingle reef like something possessed. He tore.

Somehow I got the stripped line back on the reel held the rod high and listened to the click scream its protest at the speed of the run. I stole a glance at Mary.

"I ought to wrap this pole around your head," she said in a most unladylike tone. "It was my turn . . ." But she was grinning.

That permit was still traveling, faster than any fish I've ever had on. I kept the rod high and hung on, praying he wouldn't run the leader across coral and cut it, or tangle in sea fans, get purchase, and snap it. Ten thousand horrible things that could happen crowded my mind. Now he was 600 feet away and still wide open. Then he turned a bit and ran parallel to the shore line, but still taking line, still going away. Finally he slowed, turned, and charged back toward us. I was in a sweat trying to take in the slack before it hung up on something. He roared on, our way. I reeled as fast as I could. Then just as I began to get organized, he turned and went to sea again, only to double back and come our way faster than ever. Finally he slowed and stopped, and at last I got the line tight between us. Then that snub-nosed roustabout stood on his head out there in three feet of water and started rubbing his little round snout into the sand, trying to dislodge the hook, giving the rod tip and me the shakes for fair. He had about four hundred feet of line out, and I laid back on the rod until it started to squeak. That did it. I turned him completely over, roughed him my way for ten feet before he recovered from the tumble and dashed off again. This time his rush was slower and shorter. I turned him again and kept him coming.

But suddenly Mary shouted, "Shark! Look out!" I saw the big, dark shadow of a nine foot shark chasing my fish. Goose pimples rose all over me. I took the drag off the reel, dropped the rod tip, and let the permit run

"Hit the water with the pole!" I shouted. "Bang on the side

Betty Barothy proudly displays the 12 pound grouper that took her half an hour to land.

of the boat, hard!" And I began stamping on the seat to make more noise.

Between the shark and us, we scared that permit so much he must have gone loco. He left the shark like a jet leaving a slow freight. The shark, tired of chasing bubbles, eased off seaward.

I tightened up cautiously on the line and felt the permit. Everything seemed to be all right, so I started putting the butt to him. He was tired, and I pulled him in fast, pulled him backwards, turned him over. I wanted to get him in before that great shovelnose shark changed his mind and charged again. I wanted that permit badly.

Finally I had him in close, reeled the leader to the rod tip, held the rod high, and sat on the side of the boat. I was going to tail him. I was reaching for him when Mary excitedly shoved a gaff hook under my nose.

"I'll gaff him for you," she said. "After all, I'm the guide. I want in on this."

"You've never gaffed a fish in your life," I told her. "You're not going to practice on my permit. Give me that thing."

The fish circled the boat once more, then I shoved the gaff down in the water, pulled the permit over it, and struck upwards, hard. I got him and put him in the bottom of the skiff. He weighed 19 pounds 15 ounces.

It was the night before we were to leave Rosario and head back for the Isle of Pines. We were tired. We had caught fish until they were coming out our ears. We had hardly hit the bunks before we were asleep. The next thing I knew it was broad daylight. I look at my watch. It was seven o'clock and we were supposed to have gotten under way two hours before that. We couldn't hope to reach camp before dark now.

I slid out of my bunk, walked aft. Jean and Vic were sleeping. So was Lloyd. I stuck my head through the hanging curtains. The women were gone. I hurried topside. No women. Then I noticed that one of the skiffs was missing.

Vic was at my side now. "We should have been under way two hours ago," he said. "Where are the girls?"

Just then we heard them. From back in the mangroves a quarter of a mile away, where schools of baby tarpon cruise the channels, we heard their shouts and screams. They were jumping tarpon.

Vic and I looked at each other.

"What are we doing here?" I asked. "Are we going to let a bunch of mere wives make pikers out of us?"

We grabbed us a skiff and went fishing, too.

It was 2 a.m. when we finally hit camp back at the Isle of Pines that night. We were beaten down, dead tired. A shower and nice comfortable bed looked good. Then, as we were wearily unloading, we heard those women.

"Let's go," said Virginia. "Come on."

Jean stopped his work for a minute and looked at her.

"Go?" he said. "Go where?"

"Fishing, of course," she said. "I bet there are tarpon a hundred yards from here."

And before our startled eyes, those three piled into a skiff and disappeared into the darkness heading up the river.

"At 2 a. m.!" Vic said in an unbelieving voice.

"It's a put-up job" I said. "They'll be right back."

We heard the motor stop. We heard the familiar yell that means another tarpon has jumped.

Silently we finished unloading and shuffled to our cabins. After all there is an end to all good things. If those wild-eyed women wanted to fish all day and all night too, it was O.K. with us. We slept. And it's the last time we'll ever take those dames fishing. After all, a man has to be top dog in some part of his realm.

4. Panama Payoff

The weather never smiled once—but those fish "like to ate us up"!

"CAN'T YOU COME some other time?" wrote Roy Shuey from Panama. "May's beginning of the rainy season here, and it's a bit early for big-game fishing, anyway. Another thing, no one has ever used fly or spinning tackle down here. That stuff is too light. You'd be doing everything the hard way."

Well, I wrote back that mid-May was the only time the three of us could get down to Panama during 1952. As to the light tackle, any pioneering is tough, but I'd spent most of my life pioneering such light tackle in salt water. My partners for the trip were kindred spirits. George Phillips was head of a tackle company in Alexandria, Pennsylvania, and Jean Crooks is a light tackle angler from Miami Springs, Florida.

Letters flew back and forth. Roy told us we could get charter boats in Panama for from $65 to $75 a day, including food. Round trip plane fare from Miami was $174 each. In Panama, hotel rooms ran from $5 to $15 a day. Food was inexpensive.

Finally we got the good news. Roy had arranged for a friend to take us on a four-day trip to the Perlas Islands, some thirty-five miles out in Panama Bay, on the Pacific Ocean side of the Isthmus.

Unfortunately, Roy couldn't go with us. "But let me give you a tip." he wrote. "You should really troll on this trip, because some of the biggest sailfish and dolphin in the world are near the Perlas Islands—dolphin that hit sixty pounds and sails that reach 140 and 150, even up to 200."

Troll? Anyone can do that!

George, Jean and I picked up our fifteen day tourist permits and had our smallpox-vaccination cards checked, the only formalities that were necessary for the two weeks' stay we intended to make.

We left Miami via Pan American World Airways on May 16, stopped briefly at Camaguey, Cuba, and Kingston, Jamaica, and arrived at Tocumen Airport, Panama, a little before midnight. Roy Shuey drove us to the Balboa Yacht Club. Presently he introduced us to Don Hutchison and some friends aboard Hutch's 42-foot cruiser, the Hula, on which we were to fish. The blond, wiry Hutch was a control operator at Miraflores Locks on the Panama Canal, and his friend Bill Martin was a tunnel operator at Pedro Miguel Locks. He looked big and strong enough to throw a fly a mile. With them was a short, stout, dark man, Bonarge Peregrina, a Spanish civilian employee of the army, who was going along as cook. Bonarge was a troller of note and like Hutch and Bill, gave us a pitying look when he saw our fly and spinning rods. His own outfit, we found, included a line that must have tested 100 pounds and a hook large enough to hold a whale.

Next morning as we approached the first of the Perlas string of islands, Hutch revealed that the rocky shores of Isla Pacheca had seventeen-foot tides. That looked like too much water for fly rods, so we rigged up our spinning gear. George and Jean put on underwater lures—small, round, quarter-ounce plastic plugs with a spinner in front, a set of gang hooks amidships, and a three inch feathered tail. I put on a plastic surface lure, also with a feathered tail, that popped and swam under water with a tantalizing side-to-side action.

"Too bad you had to come just at this time," remarked Hutch as he watched us rig up. "The rains have started, and you're late for the snapper and corbina. They're here in great schools in February and March. We always troll. I doubt if you fellows will do any good with those things. If you don't connect, I'll break out the trolling tackle. Of course, the sailfish season is just beginning, but you're not going to land sailfish on that tackle."

"Might get some dolphin, though," Bill suggested. "When the rainy season starts, logs and trees float down the rivers and out into the bay. Nearly always there are dolphin under them. Lots of times the driftage extends for miles, and you can cruise along it and get good fishing all the way."

These Perlas Islands hadn't changed in the more than four hundred years since Balboa, the Spanish explorer who discovered the Pacific, named them for the bumper crop of pearls that once came from their rich oyster beds.

The Hula skirted the north end of Isla Pacheca, whose tropical verdure was loaded with the nests of thousands of birds. Brown boobies flapped and soared overhead, and frigate birds also called man-of-war birds—slipped by on motionless, seven-foot wings. In the nests the half-grown young of both species stared solemnly at us.

"Hey, look!" shouted Hutch.

A hundred feet out we saw a man-of-war bird chase a booby, grab it by the tail and give it a shake. The unhappy booby pulled free, fell clumsily to the water, smoothed its feathers, and flew away. Then the frigate bird swooped down repeatedly, dipping its bill into the water.

"What goes on?" asked Jean Crooks.

"That booby had a bellyful of fish," laughed Hutch. "Dove for 'em. The man-of-war bird's a smart old cuss. When he sees a booby come up with a load, he chases it, catches it by the tail, and shakes it till it throws up. Then he dives down and gets the fish."

"The old goat!" I said.

"Very nice, but let's get fishing," I heard George growl from up forward.

Hutch obliged by maneuvering the boat to within sixty

feet of the island and turning her broadside so we could fish the shorelines.

This was it—the test of light tackle was coming up. Dropping a lure into new waters makes me tingle all over. I always expect a hundred-pounder of some mighty species to grab it at once.

"Ready, boys," I shouted. "Let's go."

Our lures hit the water simultaneously. George and Jean were letting their plugs sink when I had my hit. That fish must have been lying there waiting for the lure like a short-stop waiting for a pop fly. He caught it and then zipped across the surface, back half out, really digging. It was some kind of jack, and that meant a good long fight. I heard shouts from Jean and George; evidently they were busy, too.

My jack had sounded and was using his flat body to give my forearms a workout. I couldn't gain an inch. It was like trying to unloose the hold of an octopus tentacle. My arms felt ready to spring from their sockets. I tightened the drag. Jean landed his fish and laughed. It was a rock hind, a member of the grouper family, and about six inches long. George hoisted a two-pound hind aboard. All I could do was pump and pull while the jack kept rocking the rod tip as he shook his head and tried for the bottom.

I couldn't guess his size because you never can judge how big a jack is from his fight. A three-pounder will make you think you're hitched to a twenty-pounder. Inch for inch and pound for pound, the jack is as strong a fish as I've ever caught. Finally I landed mine—a crevalle jack. He weighed six pounds, and Hutch and Bill—even Bonarge—had to admit that maybe light tackle had its points.

Jean was shouting again. "A big one," he yelled. "Look at him go."

Line was melting off the big spinning reel and the rod was shaped like a horseshoe. Sensing a good fight, I scrambled to the bow and watched. We didn't know what it was, but it was plenty fast, and fifteen minutes elapsed before Hutch netted that fish—an 8½ pound Spanish mackerel.

"Say," said Bill sheepishly. "You fellows happen to have any extra spinning outfits handy? I believe I could learn to use one in a hurry."

"I'd like in on that, too," said Hutch.

We fitted them both out and in ten minutes they were both casting and working their lures like veterans. And both of them were getting hits, catching fish, and howling like kids.

We went on having strikes and catching fish with almost every cast. This was sport, this was what we'd come down for. Hutch would cruise along slowly, and when the tidal drift was right, he'd cut the motor. That gave us a better chance to play our lures right, and also reduced the risk of scaring fish. George and Jean cast from the bow and I stood in the cockpit. We caught about everything—Cuban, mangrove and mutton snappers; rock hind; several kinds of groupers; filefish; crevalle and horse-eyed jacks; triggerfish; hogfish; ladyfish. They all had two things in common. They were hungry and they fought hard.

We left Pacheca and ran down past Isla San Pablo, about ten acres in size and rising 23 feet above the water. As we came within casting range we got a whiff of the sultry, musty air of the jungle. Long vines wove a web over everything on the islet. Some of the taller trees had trunks so slender that we wondered how their fragile stems could hold up the top-heavy loads of branches, vines and birds. We recognized a few of the trees—gumbo limbo; frangipani with its five-petaled white flowers; mahogany; shower trees loaded with yellow, pink, and purple blossom, and trumpet trees. And over them all was draped that great green mesh of vine, as if someone had thown a vast net. Underneath was a tangle of vegetation, dying, dead and decaying. From everywhere came the sound of birds—thousands of them. The place was swarming with life.

After San Pablo we rounded Bartoleme. Here the Pacific

lived up to its name. It was still and quiet, rocking us gently with long ground swells. And then suddenly it was no longer quiet. Off to the right a school of jacks slapped viciously at baitfish. Another school showed on the left. Ahead of us we saw a big school of blue runners, two-pound fish, lying on top of the water with their dorsal and caudal fins sticking out. There were a couple of acres of them, bunched together, fin to fin. Everywhere we looked, there were surfacing fish.

And this was the off season! It was better than my best dreams had pictured it.

Hutch cut the motor and we drifted slowly towards the blue runners, ready for action. As we suspected, large fish were feeding on them from underneath, sometimes knocking the runners a foot into the air as they slashed at them, and making the great swirling boils that only a big fish can make. The moment we were near enough, I put out a long cast. The surface lure fell at the edge of the school. I gave it a pop. Then the water erupted and the plug disappeared.

I'll never know what I had on. It took off through that mass of close-packed fish and broke my line across their backs.

"Well," said Bonarge, "it's supper-time anyway."

But it was an hour before we stopped to eat. After dinner, as we lay at anchor, I noticed that Bonarge took extra care with his knot as be baited up with a snapper head.

"Once, out here," he explained, "I put de line out and someting grab de huk and zsput!" he snapped his fingers, "It's break de line. Beeg." he added. "Sometime I catch heem."

Well, Bonarge was something of a prophet. Later in the night I was awakened by a muffled struggle aft, muttered oaths, stamping feet and thuds.

I sprang from my bed, cracking my head on the bunk above, and rushed out. Bonarge, George, Jean and Hutch were all on deck, hauling on Bonarge's night line. Muscles bunched, feet braced against the stern, they were working hard but not gaining on whatever was on the other end, out there in the darkness.

12 pound Cubana snapper, taken by the author in the Perlas Islands.

"Hey, what's all this?" I asked, still half asleep.

Just then the line parted with a bang and our tug-of-war team collapsed in a heap on the deck.

"Damn!" muttered Hutch. "That was a giant manta ray. He was at least sixteen feet across. Boy, suppose he had decided to come this way."

Under the tangle of defeated anglers I saw Bonarge cross himself.

"A devilfish!" he muttered.

Next morning we fished around Isla Elefante, and George, right off, latched onto a 5¾ pound grouper. He spent a long time working that baby in. Those bottom huggers hate to come up but George finally boated it. And then no one could

figure out what kind of a grouper it was. It had big lips, and
a short, stubby, dark-brown body with faint blue lines curv-
ing here and there on its sides. I haven't been able to identify
it in any of the seven fishing books I've consulted.

George cast and was into another big one. "It's a gar, I
think," he said.

But as the fish jumped clear and skidded eight yards on his
tail, Jean and I saw its long snout and elongated, silvery body.
"A houndfish," we both yelled. "And a big one."

"They're the ones you see skipping across the surface,"
Hutch said. "If one hit you, he'd go right on through you."

That houndfish was in and out of the water, acting as if
he were trying to turn himself inside out, but luckily his
sharp teeth didn't hit the leader and finally George brought
him to the net. He weighed 7½ pounds and looked as long
as a man.

This was fishing. This was pioneering light tackle the right
way. We were having action from gamey fish, and our wispy
lines were making it sportier still. We took all we could and
kept asking for more.

We fished at Elefante and Isle de Monte all that day, landing rock hind—running from half a pound to three pounds—
until they were coming out our ears. They must have been lying on the bottom like cobblestones, because every time we let a
lure sink, one nailed it. They were a dime a dozen. We didn't
keep accurate count, but our daily count was well above a
hundred fish each. We each lost about fifteen lures a day, too,
mostly to fish that cut us off on rocks.

"I should hide my face," said Hutch. "I told you fellows
that fishing was at its worst right now. It was—but we were
trolling out here. We just watched the spot where our lines
went into the water. I got new horizons now," he grinned,
"since I started spinning."

"I got new horizons, too," I told him as I looked inshore
towards a huge downed tree, floatage that had drifted ashore.
I wondered how many dolphin had used it for an umbrella

when it was afloat. As I watched, a whitecap-topped swell rushed up the volcanic rock, reached up a hand, then a knee, and boosted its way up toward the jungle.

The surface beyond *The Hula* was alive with striking fish, and there were birds everywhere—small petrels, the ever-present boobies, man-of-war birds, and pelicans. Landside, the parrots carried on screaming conversations while smooth-billed anis, called tick birds on the Isthmus, scolded and fussed.

The number of fish in Panama waters is simply astonishing. Why? A Dutch scientist, Dr. Anton Bruun of Copenhagen University, says its because of an upswell of cooler water from a depth of 1,000 feet. Winds cause the upswell.

"It is the same phenomenon that occurs when one blows on water in a pan," says Dr. Bruun. "The water that is displaced by the wind is replaced by water that rises from the bottom. This mass of water which rises to the surface is rich in minerals; hence, rich in plant life. Because of the abundant plant life, crustaceans thrive in these waters; because of the abundance of crustaceans, fish are plentiful."

"The trade winds create the upswell," added Hutch. "They blow north and northwest across the Isthmus from January to May," he pointed out. "We always thought the big schools of corbina and red snappers came with the Humboldt Current, which swings in here at the end of February. It's then you see huge schools of corbina threshing the surface, striking into baitfish, and making a terrific noise."

"I've seen the water turn red with thousands and thousands of red snappers on the rampage," Bill put in. "It's some sight! The snappers and corbinas stay around until mid-April, when the Humboldt swings out again. That's why we always connected the two—the cold Humboldt current and the big schools of fish."

"Well, whatever brings 'em," said Hutch, "that's the time for the big schools—from Washington's birthday till the middle of April."

Later that day as we rounded a point, I saw the black,

sickle-shaped tail of a permit that was drowsing lazily on the surface. I got ready to cast, but Jean had seen him, too. He beat me to it and his lure dropped a foot in front of the fish. The great pompano surged forward, grabbed the lure, and headed east as if he intended to leap the Isthmus. He was still going a mile a minute when the hook dropped out after about 200 feet.

But we took no time for a post mortem. Jean cast again and again was fast to a fish. "Don't know what it is," he cried. "It's long and silver colored. I saw it hit. Back up, Hutch, he's taking my line."

Just then the fish turned, charged the boat, and made like he wanted to wrap the line around the propeller. Jean leaned way out, jabbed his rod under water fast, and worked him away from there. The fish ran out from under the boat, and after five more minutes of scrappy fighting, he was ready for the net. Hutch slipped it under him and brought him up, a long, slender fish that looked like a sea trout.

"A white corbina," he said.

"Looks like a California white sea bass to me," I suggested, "but I'm not sure. Both corbina and white sea bass belong to the sea-trout family."

"Whatever it is," said Bill, holding him up on the scales, "he weighs 11½ pounds."

I got my reference book from the cabin. Sure enough he was a California white sea bass, *Cynoscion nobilis*.

"*Nobilis* is right," said Jean. "He put up a noble fight."

Ten minutes later I cast a surface lure near a protruding rock. A dark red shape rose up and took. I knew it was a big snapper. I also knew it would dive for the bottom and that I'd better put the pressure on right now; if he made it downstairs he'd cut me off. I gave that eight-pound-test line more than I thought it would take. It held. But my rod handle bent slowly into a half moon under the terrific two-way pull. I kept right on horsing the fish, and in a few minutes had it in the boat—a 5¼ pound mangrove snapper. I grabbed the rod handle, bent it back into shape across my knee, and went on fishing.

On the morning of our last day we fished at Sonora Island. Abruptly the rains began to come down in great sheets, bouncing off the surface. In seconds we were drenched. But rain was so much a part of the Perlas scene that we hardly noticed it. Then, as if someone had pushed a button, it stopped —and presto, action started. We had strikes on every cast.

That day George took a 6 pound grouper, I got a 3¾ pound ladyfish and a 6 pound snapper, and Jean put the kibosh on a 4 pound horse-eye jack and a 5 pound snapper. Hutch and Bill took turns running the boat and catching fish until their arms were tired. They had to admit that this was not bad fishing for the "off season."

The last day we headed back to Balboa in time to allow a little fishing on the way in. We didn't see any of the driftage under which dolphin usually hide, but we hoped to locate a roving school of the blunt-faced acrobats. Bonarge had hung out his usual system of trolling rods and hand lines. Presently one of the reels began to click and then broke into a scream. Back of us a glistening, rainbow-hued fish burst up into the air. The whole ocean behind the boat was alive with dolphin. As far as we could see there were brilliant flashes of darting blue-and-yellow and green-colored fish.

"Keep one on out there—don't boat him!" I shouted. "The school will follow him."

Even before Hutch could cut the motors, we cast our spinning lures and all had fish on. We had dolphin bouncing in and out of the water like young quail trying to fly. They were uniform in size, a school of three-pounders. We were shouting with the excitement of it all.

Then, as suddenly as the rain had stopped, the dolphin were gone. Not a sign of life showed on the face of the ocean.

"What a country!" moaned George, wiping his brow. "What fishing!"

Then Jean, who was still up on the bow, let out a yell. "Sailfish! Two of them! Finning!"

I grabbed my spinning rod. For a moment I didn't see anything, then a sail showed back of Bonarge's bait. A second one showed behind that. I threw the plug almost on the first sail's bill, popped it once, and he took. He dived and I struck. My reel protested as that streamlined speedball felt the hook and went into high. He didn't stay with me long. Everything went slack and I rolled in the lureless line. He had cut the leader.

I turned to Bonarge in time to see him leap for his hand line, grab it, pull back, and then drop it as if he'd caught a fer-de-lance. Back of the boat a nine-foot sailfish was in the air, dancing across the surface, tail-walking up a swell. He hit the top of it and seemed to walk right on up into the air. In the corner of his mouth I thought I could see the white feather that had been on Bonarge's line.

Then he crashed down into the water and disappeared.

Bonarge was sitting in the fighting chair nursing his right hand. He held up the forefinger, showing a deep gash where the line had slashed into it. He was speechless. But he still had the strength to point that bloody finger astern.

I looked, and with shaking hands tied another surface lure on my line and threw it out.

That big sail was only twenty feet back of the boat. He took and kept right on coming. He was clear out of the water, tail-walking, catching up to us. I could see the whites of his eyes. He blotted out the sun. He was coming aboard!

Then he fell back and the line flew at me like a released rubber band. I staggered into the cabin and climbed into my bunk.

"Hutch," I called, just before burying my head under the covers, "close the hatches. Close the portholes. These fish are going to eat us up. I want to live to fish the Atlantic side. Let's hit the ball for Balboa."

FISHING TIME-TABLE, PERLAS ISLANDS, PACIFIC OCEAN,
OFF PANAMA

AMBERJACK, JACK:	All year.
GROUPER, RED SNAPPER:	All year; best from January to April.
CORBINA (CROAKER):˙	Some few all year; schools in late February and March.
CALIFORNIA WHITE OUR FISH, SEA BASS:	Some few all year; schools in February and March and to mid-April.
POMPANO:	February, March.
MACKEREL:	May to December.
BONITO, DOLPHIN, MARLIN, SAILFISH, WAHOO:	May 15 to October.

Panama has some of the biggest sailfish and dolphin in the world.

The rainy season runs from May 1 to December 1. April varies, can be wet or dry. The dry season extends from December 1 through March.

Poorest fishing months in the Pacific off Panama are November, December and January.

5. Waters Of Many Fishes

The word "Panama" means "waters of many fishes" or "abundance of fish," and the name fitted those fish-filled waters on the Atlantic side of the Isthmus.

SO FAR, we figured, Panama was rightly named, for we'd been told it means "waters of many fish" or "abundance of fish," or words to that effect. And we'd just been light-tackle fishing—George Phillips, Jean Crooks, and I—off the Perlas Islands in Panama Bay, on the west coast. Each of us must have caught 400 fish, despite the fact that this was mid-May, the beginning of the rainy season, and supposedly too early for good game angling. Now we were heading for the Atlantic side of the Isthmus to see if that also would live up to the name.

Between times, we needed a rest, so Bill Martin, who'd been with us in the Perlas, took us sightseeing along Central Avenue in Panama City—"the Crossroads of the World."

Hindus, San Blas Indians, Orientals, Europeans, and Central and South Americans were there, light-colored and dark, wealthy business men and beggars, beautiful women and slovenly slatterns. The shops enticed tourists with teakwood chests, mandarin coats, figurines, bone china, crystal, Chinese and Italian linens, Guatemalan dresses, and Swiss watches. Canny merchants, past masters in a dozen languages, stood in doorways, beckoning, eager to sell.

An Indian boy walking our way wore what looked like a

necklace of huge pearls. But they couldn't be pearls, because
the kid was eating them. Closer inspection showed that his
jewelry was a length of gelatinous, inch-wide, stringy sacs
with what looked like dark, marble-sized beans inside them.
The boy bit off a bean and chewed fast, like he was afraid
it was going to get away, then switched the necklace around,
ready for the next bite.

I look at Bill and nodded toward the boy. "What's that?"
I asked.

"Iguana eggs," Bill said. "It's a lizard, you know."

"How come?"

"Caesarean."

"Give."

"Well, it's like this. They split an iguana up the belly,
reach in and pull out her egg sac. The eggs are all yolk, soft-
shelled, and encased in transparent gut. They boil the whole
works in salt water and then put it in the sun to dry. The
natives hang the strings around their necks, and when they're
hungry, they start chawin'. It's a delicacy."

"How about the poor iguana?" Jean wanted to know.

"She recovers and goes on her way," Bill grinned. Iguana
meat is good, too, he told us. Down there it's "Panama chicken."
The natives make a dish something like Mulligan stew, and
they put everything in it but the kitchen stove. When it's
time for the iguana to go in, all the neighbours come to call.

It started to rain, but we kept on walking and everyone
else went on about his business. It rained harder, but no one
paid any attention. After all, it had been raining ever since we
arrived in Panama, and showed no signs of ever having done
anything else. But Bill told us that during the three-month dry
season from January to April, the vegetation gets so crisp and
brown that you can hear an iguana crawling a mile away.

The market stalls were loaded with exotic food. Great slabs
of white cheese lay alongside chunks of a kind of cornmeal
dough that is used in making tamales and enchiladas. In the
pet department we saw caged parrots, parakeets, love birds

and marmosets. And rising high over all—and I do mean high—was an indefinable mixture of aromas, some of them quite pleasant. But despite the smells and the masses of food openly displayed, there were remarkably few flies. Bill explained that natives butcher their meat at midnight, or very early in the morning, bring it to the market at daybreak, and sell it all before noon. That way there's no spoilage caused by the heat of the day.

Sightseeing over, we drove to the Panama Canal Tarpon Club at Gatun Dam, where we met Bill Brooks and Kenny Brassel, both small and blond and with energy written all over them, and Roy Shuey, who'd helped us to organize the trip. We were going to live for a week aboard Bill's cruiser, *The Marbella*, and fish in and around the Chagres River which joins the Atlantic at a point about eight miles west of Colon.

Bill and Kenny told me that they'd been using spinning tackle for about seven months, and that there were about eighty men on the Isthmus doing the same. The Tarpon Club has 180 members, and most are potential light-tackle spin or fly fishermen.

"You should see the snook that hit here in October and November," said Kenny. "That's when the big, sea-run fish are all over. You can take 8 to 16 pound fish any day for almost two months, and there's always a chance you may tie into a monster."

The all-tackle world-record snook came out of the Gatun Dam spillway. It was taken by Capt. J. W. Anderson, a canal pilot, in January, 1944. He was using 130-pound-test line a 6/o reel, 5/o hook, and a ladyfish for bait, and even with that tackle it took him almost an hour to land the big hulk. It weighed 50½ pounds, and was four feet seven inches long. Imagine a thing like that sticking its snout out of the water to take a popping bug!

"What are we likely to get right now?" George asked.

"Mostly tarpon, and maybe a few snappers," Roy answered. "You might run into a stray snook or ladyfish, or even a barracuda. Bill's taken a few bonefish on artificials, casting blind, but the water's too deep for good bonefishing."

Next morning, a Saturday, we made ready to board *The Marbella* at the club's dock. A lot of members were on hand stowing stuff aboard boats for a week-end's fishing. The whole place was alive with activity. Suddenly a piercing shout rang out. Everyone stopped, frozen in their tracks. It was Jean. He was standing at the end of the dock, fighting a fish.

"Ladyfish," he screamed. "Thousands of them. Everything's here—ladyfish, jacks, tarpon, snook. Hurry up."

George and I rushed to *The Marbella*, grabbed our rods, and tore back to the end of the dock. By that time it was crowded. Out in front of us breaking fish by the acre rocked the surface with their splashings.

We had lures in the air before we skidded to a stop. A tarpon of about ten pounds rolled up and swallowed my dart streamer. From the corner of my eye I saw a ladyfish jump near where George's lure landed. Shouts kept coming from Bill and Kenny on the other side of the dock. I remember thinking that it's no wonder people say fishermen are crazy. Who wouldn't be, I thought, as my fish hopped out and tossed the fly a mile high.

The dock looked like an animated cartoon. We were all casting, reeling, and fighting fish, then landing them and throwing them back. Men kept running from one side of the dock to the other. A few looked hungrily at our rods and asked questions. What kind of equipment was that? What lures? What fish were hitting? They were seasoned trollers, but our light tackle was relatively new to them. It hadn't occurred to many of them that such sport was to be had right at their own dock.

We answered the questions as best we could, and then I saw George hand his spinning rod to a fellow and start showing him how to use it; Jean did the same, and so did I, giving the men a few directions. In four or five minutes they were putting the line thirty feet out. Then a tarpon fell on a fly.

The tyro holding my favorite rod let out a yell you could have heard five miles away, pulled back with all he had, and froze.

"Take it easy!" I yelled. "You'll break him off." Just then the leader broke and the rod sprang back to a semblance of its former shape. The ex-trolling specialist turned and shoved it into my hands.

"Thanks," he said. "Thanks a lot. I'm getting one of those outfits right now." He took off for the tackle shop at the end of the dock.

Suddenly the fish went down like a curtain dropping at the end of a play, and we stood there collecting our breaths.

Then the club members started to take off downstream. Each boat, regardless of size, had a canopy on top of it. Some skiffs had large raised umbrellas. It was drizzling a bit. A couple of the boats had stout black rods set up for trolling. I'd never seen rods like them before, so I asked Kenny what they were.

"They're black palm rods," he told me. "They aren't available commercially. A few of the boys make them for the fun of it. They split the palm's outer part, like bamboo. Makes a good stiff trolling rod."

A few minutes later we got under way and headed for the mouth of the Charges, 7½ miles downstream. As we moved along the river we got our first real look at the jungle. It was thick, verdant and choked with vines. Weird-looking cannonball trees, also called monkey dinner-bell trees, grew along the shore, with fruit the size of duckpin balls hanging on long, viny stems. There were kapok trees, too, and palms loaded with huge clusters of red dates, and pampas grass twenty feet tall.

"There's a flying-ant's nest," George pointed out. It was black, four feet long and three feet around, and stuck on a tree trunk several feet up from the ground.

A procession of whitish land crabs moved steadily along the clay bank, some pausing to stare at us, and high in the tallest trees were large birds with huge curved-down bills.

"Toucans," said Roy. "They make good pets."

At the mouth of the river we tied *The Marbella* to an old dock and transferred to skiffs. On the cliff high above us were the ruins of historic Fort San Lorenzo, destroyed in 1671 by Sir Henry Morgan when he ravaged Panama, rebuilt by the Spaniards, and the object of endless raids and forays by pirates. A cannon had fallen from the parapet and lodged in the shallow water along the shoreline, four feet of its muzzle pointing skywards. After a quick look at both land and sea, we got down to business. I spotted a tarpon rolling in the channel, then saw the splash of striking fish.

"Down here tarpon feed a lot on needlefish," Roy said. "Do we have a green and white surface lure?"

We didn't, so we tied on a red-and-white, the old reliable tarpon color. As we made ready to cast, a 100-pound tarpon struck right beside the boat, throwing a bucketful of water into the skiff.

We drifted with the current, and started to cast. It was like throwing lures into a mine field, for fish exploded all around them as they lit. For thirty minutes tarpon hit fly rod streamers and poppers, and surface and underwater spin lures all equally well. We landed a few and lost a lot. Then they went down, and the surface was as flat as a lumberjack's pocket the morning after pay day.

We rowed toward the fallen cannon, intent on trying for what might lie along the shoreline. "Look," said George, "there's a hummingbird floating on the water. Must have got tired and fallen there."

I rowed over to the tiny bird and George reached out to pick it up. But just as he did, the bird zoomed into the air and flew toward the jungle. Later we saw another, and a third, and rowed over to them. Each time the same thing happened.

"They must fly out here to cool off," I suggested, "or perhaps they have lice which the salt water washes off or kills."

We fished the shoreline then, dropping surface lures on three or four feet of water, and caught mangrove snappers by the dozen. Each cast brought droves of them roaring out from the rocks, fighting each other for the lure. Some went as high as three pounds.

A strange-looking, crow-sized bird with a body like a vulture and a bright blue, hawklike head and bill flew out of the jungle and headed down river. As we followed it with our eyes, we saw that the tarpon were rolling in the channel again.

"Let's see you land one," said George.

I tied on a blue and white popping bug. Then I cast, popped the bug once, and struck. Something threw water high and immediately departed in a straight-away dash for the Atlantic. He kept on—400, 500 feet—then came out in a startling leap. He looked like fifty pounds.

"Shall I crank up and follow him?" George aked.

"Not yet. I still have some line left."

The fish reversed his course and headed our way so fast it was hopeless to try for a tight line. I hoped he was well hooked. He went seaward again and again and didn't stop until he reached the big waves where the current and the wind met. Then he came out again. I dropped my rod tip while he jumped and jumped. Finally he tired and I got him coming my way. It was tough pulling him against the fast-running water, but I kept the pressure on and George let the skiff drift. At long last I reeled him right into the maw of the landing net. He didn't hit fifty pounds, but he did weigh thirty-five.

Farther out we saw Jean and Roy.

"Jean's into a fish," said George, peering hard at them. "It's probaby another tarpon."

Fifteen minutes later the boys were still out there and Jean was standing like he'd never moved. Then we saw Roy make a dip with the big landing net, and it took both hands to haul up whatever was in it. We couldn't see how big the fish was, but they kept it.

"It's not a tarpon," I said, "or they'd have thrown it back. Must be an eating fish."

They came in then, wide open, and ran up to us. Jean

proudly held up a Spanish mackerel. It looked like a ten-pounder, but actually weighed 8½ pounds—and that's big for a Spanish.

Bill had a stack of sandwiches ready for us when we got back to *The Marbella* that night. "The meat in them is canèjo," he told us. "Canejo means rabbit. It has ears like a rat, and no hair on its feet. Some weigh as much as forty pounds. They're almost entirely nocturnal, and usually we only get a shot at them at dusk."

"Tastes something like pork," said George, chewing hard. "What else do you get in the shooting line?"

"We have the corzo," said Roy, who likes to hunt. "He's a little red deer, sometimes almost black, that weighs about fifty pounds. Has spike horns—no tines at all. We also have white-tail deer."

He said that on the ridges back in the jungle there are part-ridges and wild turkeys, and near the Chagres there are pheasants. Several varieties of doves, too.

"If you like big-game hunting, there are jaguars," said Bill. "A guy killed one just two miles from town a couple of weeks ago. Weighed 200 pounds."

Next day we fished the pool below the Gatun Dam. White water rushed in at the top and then gradually slowed and formed currents and eddies. Tarpon flashed as they rolled and worked their way into the froth. The pool was 250 feet wide and 100 yards long and looks so much like Newfoundland salmon water that I almost reached for a silver doctor instead of a big popping bug tied on a 3/0 hook. But the incessant chatter of parakeets reminded me that this was the Chagres in Panama, and not the Humber.

I cased that pool a while before starting to fish. Tarpon were in a procession, making a slow circle up through the fast water, then down through the eddy in the middle, and around and up again, lazing along. They were a long cast from where I stood. I cast for five minutes before one slurped the bug and took off for the other side of the pool. He did an oblique to the right, an about-face and busted the whole routine wide open as he came out, stood on his tail, and showed me about 150 pounds of silver. Then he shot down my way, went deep, and cut the line. Jean and Bill, who were across the pool, wiped their eyes in mock sympathy. Some Marines standing on the side of the dam raised a feeble cheer, whether for me or for the tarpon, I wasn't sure. Then we all concentrated on George.

He looked as if he were pinned against the dark gray side of the dam. He must have had the drag on his big spinning reel set mighty heavy because his rod was bent as far as it's legal for a rod to bend. He was into something big. I joined the spectators out there with him. Some kids passing by waded out near him.

"A big snook," George gasped.

The fish did a heavy roll 100 feet out in the fast water, and snatched ten yards of line before George could stop him. He came halfway out, showing his long snout and heavy shoulders.

"Take it easy, George," I shouted. "He's too good to lose."

George knew just what he was doing and how much his equipment would stand. Even so it was half an hour before he skidded that baby up on the cement below the dam's apron. It weighed twelve pounds.

Later we went back to the Tarpon Club docks, remembering the fun we'd had before leaving for the Chagres, and wanting to try it again. A slough to the left of the docks looked good to us. It was rimmed with water cabbages. At the end of it was a small creek. Kenny said that during the snook run lots of big ones were taken there. We boarded three skiffs and headed for it.

We'd only gone 100 yards from the docks when the surface busted as a school of fast-traveling jacks moved in. I dropped my spinning lure in front of them, and got a hit immediately. Kenny did the same.

We each pulled in a 2 pound jack crevalle, and put them back. Then a tarpon rolled. We both cast at that, and again we wound up with two fish on, tarpon this time. They didn't stay long. But fish were showing all around. Kenny landed a 4 pound horse-eye jack, and I boated a 4 pound ladyfish.

As we drifted along, I noticed two natives trolling with hand lines from a skiff. As they threw the lines over, I saw the splash of a big spoon.

"Commercial fishermen," Roy explained. "They catch ladyfish, tarpon and snook."

"I never heard of anyone eating tarpon or ladyfish," I remarked. "Ladyfish are full of bones."

The natives like them both, he explained. "They dig the meat out of ladyfish with a spoon, to avoid the bones, and make it into fish cakes."

The commercial men had been watching us, and not catching a thing. When Kenny nonchalantly released a thirty pound silver king that had kept him busy for half an hour, the men went wild. They leaped to their feet, twirled their spoons around their heads, threw them as far out as they could, and retrieved them in foot-long jerks. Soon one of them yanked in a 5 pound tarpon.

We cranked up and ran for the creek entrance. Roy cut the motor a quarter of a mile out, Kenny rowed in, and we went along the shoreline.

The creek's mouth was about five yards wide, with water cabbages on either side and a few floating in the middle. A tree limb stretched across the opening only four feet above the water. It was going to be tough casting, but the place sure looked fishy.

Minnows were jumping about 100 yards away, showering up by the dozen as bigger fish below struck into them. The whole surface suddenly exploded. It was a wild, fierce display of savage, hungry fish. They knocked the minnows into the air and seemed to grab them on the fly. So many fish were breaking that we couldn't hear each other speak. We had to yell.

We sat there and looked for a while, then went into action. Every cast was a hit. We caught ladyfish, snook, jack crevalle, horse-eye jack, snappers, and tarpon. I'd never seen or caught so many different kinds of fish together. It lasted half an hour and was the wildest, fastest angling I'd ever done. Then, like magic, there weren't any fish. All gone.

I washed the slime off my hands, wiped the sweat from my brow, and turned to Roy and Kenny. "You say you fellows don't ever fish here?"

"Maybe it's too close to the Club," said Kenny. "Most of the members go trolling. All this is new to them. Bill and I have been catching fish like this on fly and spinning gear, but it wasn't until the fellows saw us on the dock the other day that they realized how much fun there is in light tackle. The tackle shop's sold forty spinning and fly outfits in three days."

We saved the last day of our stay in Panama to fish the jungle rivers that run into the Chagres. *The Marbella* dropped George and me at the mouth of one river, and the others went on to try another not far away.

We rowed our skiff around a bit before starting to fish. A royal blue butterfly with wings at least four inches wide batted his way up the river ahead. He lifted six inches with each wing beat. A water possum swam across in front of us. Off in the jungle a partridge kept calling, then another joined him. They kept trying to run the scale, but they never made the eighth note.

Suddenly George set his rod down and put his head in his hands.

"I feel awful," he said. "Hot all over, and my eyes burn."

"Maybe you've got malaria," I worried helpfully. "We'd better go back. Let's rest a minute, anyway."

I eased the boat into the shade, and we sat there a few minutes. Then, as I watched, a shaft of sunlight flickered through the leaves. "George," I said, "let's get the hell out of here and go fishing."

He looked startled. I pushed the boat out. "We're dopes," I said. "The sun's shining for the first time since we came to

Panama, and no wonder you are hot and your eyes hurt. So do mine."

George's worried frown turned into a big smile. He picked up his rod.

As we moved along, a five-inch kingfisher, black all over, with a white slash on each shoulder, flew beside us, then settled on a dead limb sticking out of the water. We passed within arm's length of him and he looked us right in the eye.

"He doesn't know any better," George laughed. "If he knew we were human beings he'd have taken off and not stopped short of the San Blas Islands."

The river we were on was about thirty feet wide and three feet deep, but along its banks were deeper holes. George cast into one, let the lure rest for a moment, then gave it a twitch. The surface opened wide enough to let a snook's mouth through. He wasn't too big so George was able to turn him before he could get under the bank and break off. He weighed about three pounds.

We heard a wild turkey yelp, and we both yelped back. Maybe we didn't do so good, because suddenly the jungle was still. But soon a howler monkey came swinging through the trees, stuck his face out at us, then beat it. Later, far off, we heard a troupe of them talking over the situation. In a few minutes the jungle echoed with the chattering and scolding of innumerable parrots.

"Parrots pair for life," George said.

"Sounds like they all have nagging wives," I commented.

With that we returned to our fishing, and began to catch fish regularly. They averaged between five and six pounds, and that's class AA in any angler's league.

"Should be a big one in there," I said, pointing to where a feeder stream emptied into the river.

George made a bullseye. That snook must have had his mouth open. He took at once, charged, went under the boat, and jumped on the other side. George dipped the rod and steered the line around the stern and clear of danger. The snook tried for a mass of stumps twenty feet away.

"Keep him away from those roots," I shouted.

"Look at my rod," George answered.

It was bent nearly double. The reel's drag was set so heavy it pulled the big fish to the surface where it fought with its dorsal in the air. It gave ground, backward, and George pulled it all the way around. I thought he had him then, but that snook dived under the boat again and high-tailed it for the creek. He reached it, too, and went out of sight, but George stopped him and pulled him back. After that he tired fast, and at last I slipped the net under him. I could scarcely wait to get him on the scales. He went 16 pounds 11 ounces.

"That's a fine way to end our trip, George," I said. "Let's go back to *The Marbella*."

All too soon we were climbing aboard the cruiser and heading upriver for the Club dock. I went below to freshen up.

It had been a great fishing trip, I reflected as I put the finishing touches to my necktie and ran a comb through my hair in preparation for the drive to the airport. A glance in the mirror made me feel like a dude. But after all, a guy has to go home sometime, and we just had time to make it to the Pan American Airlines terminal.

I was struggling into my sport coat when an ear-splitting scream tore through the night air. I froze. I heard that yell again.

This time I didn't hesitate. I rushed for *The Marbella's* deck, grabbed my rod from topside with my free hand, shook the coat off, and was ready to cast.

"Fish!" Jean was yelling. "Fish by the thousands!"

6. Northern Lights Fish

Seeking the grayling, the fish with an angel's wing for a dorsal, from the Yukon to the mountain lakes and streams of Montana.

"I WONDER how they got such a beautiful dorsal?" said my friend Gene Letourneau. He was holding up an Arctic grayling that he had just pulled from the Yukon River.

"That's easy," I answered. "Thousands of years ago the first grayling was swimming in primeval darkness. Suddenly a great light shone in the skies, blazed and then faded, then burst out again in many colors. The grayling rose to the surface for a better look, and his dorsal fin stuck out. The northern lights looked down at that drab bit of fish flesh. "A pity," they said. "Such a dull-looking fish. Let's light him up." And like a flash they swept down and painted that grayish-hued fish with their own colors."

"And the grayling thanked the northern lights," grinned Gene, "and swam away to take a dry fly."

The grayling is the fly-takingest fish of them all. He goes for flies as a Scandinavian goes for coffee. All you need to do to catch one is put a fly on the end of your leader tippet and cast thirty feet out into any of the waters in which he lives. Maybe it's the short feeding season in the cold northern water which is his natural habitat. Perhaps it's because the limited amount of food other than flies and nymphs in this water has conditioned him to flies. Or maybe he just prefers flies over

65

other catchable items, the way a kid prefers candy. Whatever it is that gives him his ravenous appetite, a grayling is always ready. He greets a fly like a long-lost relative.

My first encounter with the Arctic grayling took place with-in the city limits of Whitehorse in the Yukon Territory. Bill Ackerman, Jack Mahony and I all from Miami, drove shiveringly out to the Lewes River, a branch of the Yukon, and stopped to fish in sight of the famous gold-rush town.

"What are grayling like?" we asked Sam McBride, local outdoor scribe, who was showing us around. "How do they act?"

"Like houseflies to flypaper," he grinned. "They hit often and get stuck."

"How big do they go?" asked Jack.

"Seldom over two pounds," Sam replied. "But in some spots here and in Alaska, too, they run as high as six pounds. The average right here will be about fourteen inches."

The river was a hundred feet across, and the pool that Sam had chosen for us was a good three hundred yards long, clear and slick as a mirror. Fish were dimpling all over it, sending out concentric circles. It seemed as if a gentle rain were falling, so numerous were those rises. I gave myself a shake. This was it—the dream of a lifetime, coming true.

On the advice of Sam, we had all tied on size 12 Black Gnat dry flies. Before I even got mine in the air I heard simultaneous shouts from my two fishing pals. They were both into fish. In the quick glance I shot their way I saw water splashing and the flash of Jack's fish as it jumped clear. Then I jerked my head back and started casting.

When my Black Gnat dropped, it didn't even have time to shake the water off its hackles before a grayling had it. I struck and was busy with a good fish. It darted around, jumped into the air, thrashed on top, ran my way, and finally slowed down enough to let me skid him into my landing net. He was *Thymallus signifer*, the Arctic grayling, largest and most color-ful of the whole family. He was 16 or 17 inches long and his big dorsal stood up like a sail, three inches long and almost as high.

I marveled at the color. It was purple-tinged, with a jagged line of rose along the top edge, and overall were numerous dark-blue dots, all circled in pink rings. Beneath that, his body was cigar shaped, whitish, with black dots on either side along the shoulders, and the whole thing just faintly tinged with brown. He had unusually large eyes for his size and a small mouth that opened in a square O as I took out the hook. I held him up to my nose for a brief sniff of the thyme odor that gives them their scientific name, then popped him back into the water. We wanted grayling to eat that night, but this was my first, and too pretty to kill. He gave a grateful flip of his tail and swam away.

My next cast got an immediate strike, and I missed. The force of the strike jerked the fly my way a couple of feet, and when it stopped another grayling was there to nab it. I missed again and then started to strip the line back for the next cast. As I raised the rod tip, still another fish socked that fly just as it was leaving the water, and I pulled that one clear out. But it fell back in again, free, and then, as I started to recover line again, I had still another hit, and this time fought it out with what proved to be a fine, fat and able 14-incher.

After ten minutes of that kind of fishing, I took a quick look around to see that no one was watching to question my sanity. Then I took off that Black Gnat and tied on a Dark Montreal, wet, on a No. 12 hook. I was trying to find a fly they wouldn't hit so hard!

But that one didn't do any better. It had hardly touched the water when one of those hungry grayling with the neon dorsals climbed aboard. They tore it into shreds. And no matter what I offered them, it was the same. Once in a while I would stop for a breather and look around. It was cold and still. I remembered some Robert W. Service: "And the icy mountains hemmed you in with a silence you most could hear."

It was like that now, still and quiet, with only the liquid

voice of the water running over pebbles along the shore behind me. Although it was early September, the thermometer already read 19 above. Across the river I could see snow on the peaks above timberline. The water was icy and I was chilled to the bone. Only the gold and yellow and brown of the changing aspens, vivid splotches against the somber pines, fed some warmth to my eyes. The·cottonwoods along the river were colored up, too, and between them the river ran deep, cold blue, shot with purple and here and there the reflected gold of the aspens and cottonwoods. No wonder grayling liked to live here.

Then I heard voices and Jack and Bill were in back of me, waving and telling me to come ashore. Time to get back to the Whitehorse Inn, and that grayling dinner. It was tough to wade out and leave a pool full of rising fish, but my tingling legs and deadened toes told me I was ready to look up a roaring furnace. There would be more fishing tomorrow. Meanwhile we got warm enough to do a job on three plump grayling apiece and found they were just about what many people claim—easily one of the best eating of all the fresh-water fish.

During that brief Alaska-Yukon trip, anglers in our party caught plenty of grayling almost everywhere they fished. In those northern waters they cover a wide range, occurring in every major drainage system north of the Gulf of Alaska. They are found in British Columbia, the Yukon Territory, are common in most of the Alaska Peninsula and in the Bristol Bay and the Kuskokim watersheds. They are in all the fresh-water clear streams along the Arctic Coast from the mouth of the Yukon to Demarcation Point. They thrive in the tributaries of the Yukon and cause angler traffic jams in the big river itself. They do well in the Tanana, Koyukuk and Kantishna. Wherever they are found, they seek the crystal-clear streams and shun those that run milky with glacial silt.

In those cold northern waters they are in a semi-dormant condition for a period of at least five months, while snow and ice close them in, not eating, just putting in time till the spring

The author with an arctic grayling, in the Yukon River near Whitehorse. The enlarged dorsal, badge of this beautiful species, was 2¼ inches long and 2¼ inches high.

breakup. When ice-out occurs, they go on a feeding spree which makes you wonder where they pack it all, and which, in short order turns them into a little fish with a big paunch.

During the same trip, Gene Letourneau and I had a field day with better than average grayling at Otter River Falls. Those we had caught in the Yukon and its tributaries had averaged about 14 inches, but up here, 125 miles north of Whitehorse and ten miles off to the east from the Alcan Highway, they went several inches better, although our biggest grayling from each river measured the same, 18 inches.

Viv Gray of Cleveland, and Ham Brown of Baltimore were fishing with us, too, and having plenty of sport, and that day

Ham landed what proved to be the prize rainbow of the trip. But we were so busy with grayling that we could hardly take time out to watch the fight, even though that rainbow did tricks that made his scales fly through the air. We had no time for anything but those hard-hitting fish with the angel's wing for a dorsal. This was the first time we had been able to get into them, and it might be the last.

But that shows how wrong you can be. It was only a year later that I waded out into a Montana stream in search of *Thymallus signifer tricolor*, the Montana grayling.

Originally grayling were found in both Michigan and Montana as well as the Yukon and Alaska areas. Because of their willingness to swat a fly, plus fishing pressure and the gradual over-all warming of the rivers there, the Michigan grayling is now extinct. The Montana species was native only in the Missouri River above Great Falls, but now has been transplanted to many other localities in the state, notably in some Yellowstone Park waters, the Big Hole River in south-western Montana, and the Belly River in Glacier Park. They are numerous in high mountain lakes and in other streams, too, where cold water prevails year round, yet where, for the two-week season required for the eggs to hatch, the water temperature goes above 50 degrees. Planted in such places by the Montana Department of Fish and Game, they are spawn-ing naturally and doing well. But if left alone, unaided by creel limits and seasons, and where fishermen in numbers could get to them, they would be caught out in a hurry.

The same thing holds true in other states, such as Wyoming, to which Montana grayling have been introduced. Because of their willingness to take a fly, only three things can assure their continuance in goodly numbers: rigid supervision by the state fish and game departments, the shortness of the season during which anglers can fish for them, and the remoteness of the waters in which they thrive.

The newcomer to grayling waters will have no trouble in identifying his catch. The Montana grayling, while not as vividly colored as the Arctic member of the family, has the same bluish head with a bronze tint over it, and his back is purple and blue blending into silvery sides, with black-dotted shoulders. So far he might possibly be confused with the Rocky Mountain whitefish that occurs in many of the same streams, but when you reach the dorsal fin, all confusion ends. The grayling fin stands up purple and green, edged with that eighth of an inch of jagged rose, and is lined with purple and blue dots, some showing faint circles of green and yellow. They do not grow as large as the more northern grayling, ranging mostly around eight and nine inches, with an occasional one that reaches fourteen inches.

The upper waters of the Big Hole River, between Wisdom and Jackson, are literally teeming with these little fish with the big fin. On my first trip there John Krause of Jackson, who knows the surrounding meadows like his own back yard, directed us across fields and around irrigation ditches till we were completely lost. But John, with an uncanny eye for landmarks, knew where we were.

"You want grayling," he said. "Well, I'll take you where I know you'll get grayling. Plenty of them."

The Big Hole ran for miles through those great meadows, meandering along with riffles and four-or-five-foot-deep pools, slipping past banks where over-hanging bushes provided ideal cover for fish. It wasn't more than fifty feet across anywhere, a far different river than down lower where I had fished it for brownies and rainbows.

The first pool we chose was slick and clear, and fish were rising all over it. Here and there we saw a snout stick up as a fish took a natural. Bill Browning, who was with me, wanted pictures for a movie he was working on, and if ever there was a natural spot where you could be sure of photogenic, real-acting fish, this was it. While Bill set up his camera I edged in at the bottom of the 100-foot pool. I made a false cast and dropped the fly about four feet above where I had seen a rise. The float had hardly started when the water opened up and two six-inch fish jumped out, one on either side of the fly, collided in mid-air and fell back in.

"Shucks!" said Bill from the bank. "I wasn't quite ready."

"Well, I can't promise you that again," I said. "Even with grayling."

I turned back to my fishing just in time to see a fish take my still-floating fly, a size 16 Black Gnat. I set the hook and the rod tip stayed down. This was no 6-incher. This was a heavy fish with lots of gumption. He slashed away to the right and then came out in an end-over-end jump. It was a grayling about 14 inches long, and his sail was flapping in the breeze. He went away so fast and strong that I had to give him line. Again he jumped, and then went deep and lay there in the current, trying to rest up a bit. But I hauled back on the rod and pulled him off his couch, and after a couple more half-hearted tries at jumping, he gave in. I skidded him into the landing net, took the hook out and held him up for the camera, then put him back.

"I think I got him on the jump, with that fin up," said Bill. "That sure is a beautiful fin. I wonder what its purpose is."

"Probably uses it to swim with," I suggested. "But more likely, from its coloration I'd be inclined to think it might be a nuptial thing—an attraction for the other sex. It probably becomes brighter just before and during the spring spawning season."

"They sure fade fast when the fish dies," Bill observed. "But I've noticed something I've never known to be true of any other fish. Even when a grayling is dead and has faded, if you put him back in the water for a minute or two, all that vivid color flares up again."

Fish were so thick in that pool that in a short time Bill had all the pictures he needed. "Now I'll fish," he said, stowing the camera.

"Let's fish together," I suggested. "Two strikes and out."

"Good enough," he agreed.

We worked slowly upstream, fishing the same pools, taking

In the Upper Big Hole River, near Wisdom, Montana, a grayling hits a dry fly.

turns. Bill started and caught four fish before he missed two strikes in a row. It was my turn. I missed two strikes in a hurry and dropped back to make way for the other team. Bill took three fish this time, then missed a couple of fish.

I held up a size 18 Light Cahill I had just tied on. "I won't miss so many strikes now. That size 12 hook I was using is a bit too big for these small fish."

"This fly should hook them better," I added as I shot it out over the pool.

It worked, too, I caught three fish, then missed two strikes. Bill caught five more. I caught four in a row.

"This is fun," I finally declared, "But I'm going to put on a size 10 fly and try for a big fish."

"Me too," said Bill. "We'll change the rules. We'll take

turns until we catch a good fish, and then it's the other fellow's pool."

I made several casts, and each time small swirls bubbled under the big fly. One larger fish knocked it an inch into the air. I threw the next cast in where the water ran deep-looking against the far bank and watched it ride the current, just a couple of inches out. I had a hit and knew it was the big one I was looking for. I struck hard, set the hook and yanked a 5-inch grayling out of the water. He literally flew our way, missed Bill by an inch and fell in the pool in back of us.

"You should be ashamed," said Bill. "Manhandling a little fish like that."

"I thought it was at least a five-pounder when it hit," I grumbled.

Once more the fly started on its journey and once more a fish came up and swallowed it. I struck with a gentle, uplifting motion of the rod this time and was into another nice fish. He was a grayling, and he bounced out obligingly and gave me a look at the whole fourteen inches of him, then headed for a hole under the bank. But I held on, and the rod tip absorbed his rush, pulled him back. I played him for another four or five minutes before I brought him to net.

This was certainly a great spot for grayling. Farther down the Big Hole the previous year I had run into a few of them scattered among the big browns and rainbows, but this was their home ground. Every cast brought a strike. Occasionally it would be an eastern brook, up to a pound, and now and again a rainbow, but basically this was grayling water. They were five to one over other fish in that part of the stream.

That seems to be the way in most waters where they do thrive. At the famous fishing town of Dubois, Wyoming, I asked Duane Redman if there were any grayling within reach.

"Lake of the Woods is full of them," he said. "It's a long, tough trip, so be ready early."

The lake was high up in the mountains, so high that it was tough going even for a jeep. We went up and up, over precip-

itous slopes that would daunt a chimney sweep, over rivulets
and rivers and snow banks and mountain divides. Duane took
that mountain-goat-on-wheels through some places that would
have scared the pants off a space cadet. But although we
couldn't walk for a few minutes after dismounting, we finally
did make it, pumped up the rubber boat we had brought,
and shoved out into the lake.

The surface was dimpled with rising fish, and those grayling
acted just like grayling should. They climbed aboard the
familiar Black Gnats as fast as we could drop them on the
water. We caught fish steadily for an hour, nice fat grayling
running between nine and fourteen inches. They were full
of pep and as willing as anyone could wish. Then around the
middle of the morning they suddenly laid off. We went ashore,
ate and rested up before starting out again to see if we could
waken those drowsy fish. For half an hour we had poor luck.
But suddenly, as if someone had rung a bell, the surface broke
into a thousand dimples. The fish were up. A grayling just
can't stay down for long. We took them on light Cahills,
size 16. We took them on an Adams, size 14, and even caught
some on a Gray Hackle, size 20. We tried nymphs and they
worked, too. We used ants and they were good. Those wild-
eyed bozos hit everything we showed them.

While grayling, both the Arctic and the Montana varieties,
will take almost anything you show them, when they go
down during the midday heat, or when the barometer is off,
or when fishing pressure has scared them from the surface,
it takes a bit of figuring to decide what type of fly to use.
Then there are certain flies that pay off in the long run. Over
the years, the black flies have proved best, the Black Gnat,
the Black Flying Ant, the Black Hackle, and even a Black
Bivisible have been high up on the list of strike bringers. They
seem to prefer darkcolored nymphs, too, although the Gray
Nymph is always good, and the yellow one frequently.
Beetles in black and brown finishes do well. When those lusty

grayling are in the mood for blondes, the Light Cahill and the Brown Hackle and Royal Coachman will do the job.

All the flies should be tied on hook sizes 18 to 12, because, despite the avidness of its strike, the grayling has a small mouth and is difficult to hook. With the small flies, I like a light outfit, a 7½-foot rod that weighs 3 to 3½ ounces or an 8-foot rod weighing up to four ounces. The line should match the rod—an HEH for the smaller one, and an HDH for the 8-footer. Leaders should be nine feet long and tapered to a 4X terminal point.

This past summer I fished the grayling waters near Jackson again, with Howard Cox of Cincinnati.

"I've never seen a grayling," Howard told me as we put our rods together. "Do you think I'll get one?"

"Well," I said, "You know how fish are. Sometimes they just won't hit. "But," I hastened to add, "if you don't catch one here, and right away, I won't wet a line all day."

We walked to the first pool.

"I'll stay with you till you catch your first one," I said. "Then I'm going fishing, too."

The surface was covered with dimples, and Howard took a ten-inch grayling on his first cast. I departed on the run for the next pool.

Later in the day we met up again. I stood and watched Howard. He was laying out a beautiful line, dropping the fly on a dime, having strike after strike. Yet, as I watched, seven fish struck, made fights of varying lengths, threw the hook, and got off. He wasn't performing the way he had when I left him.

"What's the trouble?" I asked, wading out beside him. "How come so many get away?"

Howard turned a big wide grin on me and held up his fly. "I cut the barb off," he said. "I'm catching so many and I'm afraid of hurting them."

"Me, too," I said, holding up mine.

We kept just enough for dinner, took them to the Diamond

Bar Inn and had the cook fry them for us. After we had laid down our knives and forks, we leaned back, as relaxed and happy as it's possible for a fisherman to be when not in a trout stream.

"Where else ——" began Howard.

I was ready for him.

" 'There's a land where the mountains are nameless and the rivers all run God knows where ——' "

"The Yukon, eh?" mused Howard. "You've been there?"

"Yep," I said. "And do you remember? 'And I want to go back and I will.' "

7. Tumble Rocks!

Adventure with a mighty salmon at the foot of the famous falls of the Humber River, Newfoundland.

ON THE GANDER RIVER in Newfoundland, I saw a run of fresh salmon come into the Joe Beggs Pool. I noticed their splashing down in the rapids below, then saw them come greyhounding toward me. A couple of them jumped high, as if in joy at striking the quiet water. Near the middle of the pool one came out clear on a 40 degree slant, then bellywhopped in again. In back of him, another sloshed along the top for two lengths.

The salmon I had been working on must have heard them coming. He jumped out, too, a long, deep fish with a caudal as broad as an axe blade. Then the main body of those fish hit him and he busted out on a bee line for the rapids above. The speeding pack chased after him.

I knew that if I could have caught one, the tiny sea lice that only live 24 hours in fresh water would still be on him. And maybe his sides would show net marks, or there would be scars to show where he had leaped into the face of a falls and banged hard into the rocks, or he might have a gash from a marauding seal. This was their first wild, thrilling run from the sea. They were strong and bright from the salt and they wouldn't stop until they reached some special pool, perhaps miles above, where they would settle down for a week, or a month, or two months, until some insistent, internal clamoring drove them on again, up and up, to shallower water, to gravel beds to spawn.

I was almost sure there wasn't a salmon left in the pool after that wild parade, but just to be certain I made a cast. There was a swirl and I struck and yanked a five-inch salmon parr right out of the water. I wet my hand, took the parr off the hook and placed it gently back in the river. It would be three or four years at least before that "peel" of the salmon would be charging upstream like the wild ones that had just rolled through. Meantime, he would live in the river, feeding on flies, growing stronger for two or three years until he was ready to go to sea. And some day, out there, maybe in three years, maybe in five—no one knows for sure—he would feel the pull of home, and then, from out there in the salt, it would be his time to return to the stream where he was bred.

Some anglers think that it is the memory of his parr days that makes an adult salmon hit a fly; for even though they take artificials, and poachers are known to have caught them on worms, their stomachs are empty whenever they are taken in fresh water and it is commonly believed that they do not eat after they leave the salt.

Whatever the reason, the Atlantic salmon hits a fly with such abandon, mixed with such discretion, that he is regarded by many as the top game fish. To take salmon consistently, and, in fact, any way but accidentally, you must know the country and the river and the pool you are fishing.

Newfoundland is a small fly country, and flies tied on anything larger than a number 4 hook are seldom needed. The bigger flies are used during the run-off of snow water in the spring, but in Newfoundland the rivers are usually low and clear by July 1st, and they keep dropping until only the low water flies on small hooks, or even small trout flies, will take fish.

To take a really large salmon on one of these small flies is the thrill of a lifetime. One of Newfoundland's oldest guides, Micmac Indian Jim Johns, tells of fishing a 75-year-old doctor who took a 44-pound salmon from the Gander—the largest ever taken on that river—on a size 12 Cowdung, a trout fly.

Standing high on the cliff, angler looks out over the Big Falls of the Humber River. Salmon can often be seen jumping up the face of the falls.

The doctor fought that fish from 6 p.m. until midnight, and they followed it upstream for 2½ miles. They landed and Jim built a fire while the doctor worked the fish in. At last it was ready for the net. Jim reached—and there was a hole in the net and the big salmon went on through. Finally the doctor brought the fish in again, and this time Jim jumped on it, drove his hunting knife into it, and carried it ashore.

Some of the best wet flies to use in Newfoundland waters are the silver doctor, silver grey, mar lodge, blue charm, logie, black dose, black doctor, Jock Scott, dusty miller, Cosseboom, and the March brown. The moosehair flies, tied locally, have paid off recently in Newfoundland. The wing is made of moosehair but otherwise they follow the body pattern of the regularly tied salmon flies. Some use jungle cock but there seems to be a movement to defrock that feather, and New-foundlanders claim they catch just as many salmon without it. The moosehair flies are certainly cheaper and as they are equally effective, it looks as if they will take over the New-foundland market.

There are three flies that make salmon mad, or so it seems from the way they charge them: the thunder and lightning, the green highlander and the Durham Ranger. On my first trip to Newfoundland, I fished Petrie's Rock Pool on the Gander with Roy Petrie of Grand Falls, after whose father the pool is named. Roy handed me a Durham Ranger.

"This one makes them see red," he said.

And it did. On my first cast for Atlantic salmon, a fish shot up, mouth open like he was going to take me instead of the fly. I was too frozen to strike, which was probably just as well, because I would have pulled his head off. Anyway, he had it and was down through the pool and into the next one before I could speak.

But there was nothing wrong with Roy's voice, and to the tune of "Keep the tip up, drop the tip, let him go, watch out!" I fought that fish in and finally landed a five-pound grilse. I sat and looked at him for a long time—a thorough-bred of the river, spawned from a long line of silvery thunder-bolts, a steeplechaser with countless water barriers behind him.

"A grilse," explained Roy, indicating the forked tail. "When he's a salmon, his tail will be square. In Newfoundland, we class six pounds and under as grilse."

In Newfoundland waters, the sizes most needed in wet flies are 8 and 10. Some anglers still use the double-hooked wet flies but, like the big, heavy, two-handed rods, that type of hook is on the way out. The single hook drops lightly, holds better, and swims better than the larger, heavier ones.

When the water warms and drops, the dry fly comes into its own. The best patterns are the grey Wulff, the brown Wulff and the royal Wulff, with the white Wulff occasionally getting results. The big hair flies float well and show up well, in sizes 6 to 12; and other good dries are the grey hackle, the grey hackle with red body, the brown hackle, the brown and also the black bivisibles. The hair-bodied flies in grizzly, grey and ginger are good. There are dozens of dry flies that will bring hits from salmon, but with dries, it's the shape of the fly, and the way it rides down the current that count, and therefore a large selection is not necessary.

All the salmon flies in the world will not help you if your trip doesn't coincide with the run of fish in the river. Usually the date of the run varies only a day or two from year to year, but occasionally natural conditions will hold the fish back, as in 1954 when an unusually large number of icebergs in White Bay and elsewhere along the Newfoundland coast delayed them as much as ten days. It also pays to know the place where the fish stop on their first drive upstream.

For instance, salmon enter the Humber River about June 20th and don't stop, or come within the angler's reach, until they come to the Big Falls Pool, 20 miles above the town of Deer Lake. Once they reach there, the fishing is fabulous. In late July they begin to stop in all the pools and the Lower Humber holds some monster fish, mostly above 20 pounds.

Salmon come into the Serpentine on the west coast of Newfoundland also about June 20th and run up to the first falls before stopping. On the Gander they make the run about the end of June and don't stop until they hit the pools immediately below the town of Glenwood. On South Brook the first salmon is usually caught about June 27th, and the same date goes for nearby West Brook and the Indian River, both of which empty into Hall's Bay.

A bright day is bad news for the salmon angler. From 1 p.m. until 6 p.m., particularly, when the sun is on the pools, the salmon will lie in plain sight, their snouts in back of a rock. Then it seems as if nothing will make them rise. Once at Grant's Pool on the Serpentine, when I was alone, I decided to try a "kill or cure" medicine. I went ashore, picked up a couple of rocks about the size of tennis balls, and threw them into the tail of the pool. Then I walked up and tossed two more rocks into the fast water at the top.

Ten pound salmon floats down over the falls in East River in New-foundland, while the angler plays him very gingerly on a 4 pound test tippet.

I waited a couple of minutes up there and then started a series of casts. On the third float, a salmon took, careened up, shattered the surface into a thousand jigsaw pieces, and threw the hook. Then at the tail, at the drop off, I saw another one rise.

I hitched on a size 10, low water silver doctor and skidded it across his snout. He grabbed it the first time and hopped out, and I dropped the rod tip as that acrobatic broadjumper covered eight feet in a going-away leap. He hit and bounced right away, and once again I dropped the tip. I didn't want him to fall on my three-pound-test tippet and break it; nor did I want him to get a straight-away pull, because then a sudden charge or jump would snap the leader. If he was well hooked, the slack I was giving him didn't matter; and if he wasn't well hooked, it wouldn't matter anyway. But he didn't get off, and at last I got him into dead water and skidded him up on shore. He was a sleek fourteen-pounder, a bright fish that woke up hungry when he was rocked.

During the first few days on the stream, almost every novice salmon fisherman, and many an expert, loses more fish on the strike, than he hooks. Salmon don't always take with a rush. They ease up on the fly and suck it in, or they take it so quietly that you think a parr is there instead of an older member of the family. If you delay the strike, they will hook themselves. And with either wet or dry flies, it pays to wait until you feel the fish before striking. But it's tough to wait and it's easy to get excited, strike too fast, and lip the fish.

Once, on South Brook, I saw a couple of salmon rising in the tail of a pool I was just starting to fish. I went below, tied on a size 8 grey Wulff and started casting. On my first float, the fly had a bit of drag and I saw three salmon, one after the other, come up for the fly, refuse, and sink down. My fingers started to do a tap dance on the rod grip and when the first salmon busted out at the fly on my next cast, I struck so fast he couldn't even get to it.

I was shaking up a fit, now, so I made myself walk away to rest the pool and try to get a grip on my jumpy nerves. Three minutes later I went back and struck too fast again. But I felt the fish this time. I was doing a bit better.

I figured there was still that third salmon that I hadn't scared, so I pulled two extra feet of line off the reel and made the cast. I didn't touch that extra line as I guided the fly over the fish with my right hand holding the rod, my left hand well away from the line. When the fish took, I couldn't snatch the fly away, for there was that two feet of slack. And when it came tight, the hook went home and I had a seven-pound salmon.

In small streams, like South Brook, you must go fine in tackle and fish the pools quietly. A fifteen-foot leader tapered to a 4-foot section of 4-pound test nylon will fall lightly and not scare the fish. For, contrary to what many fishermen believe, salmon do scare, and though they may stay right in plain sight, once you've scared them they're as down as a broken elevator and you can't raise them with a drag line, much less a fly line.

More and more $8\frac{1}{2}$-foot rods with HCH line to match, and with long, light leaders are showing up on salmon streams in place of the old, two-handed, heavy outfits. It makes for more strikes, more fun, and a fairer break for the salmon, though I sometimes wonder if they need a break, any break at all. They can do things to you that no other fish can do. Like the one I hooked more recently.

We were fishing the Big Falls Pool on the Humber, classed since time unremembered as one of the greatest salmon pools in the world. The first three days were too bright for good fishing. Each day we took a few grilse in the morning, and again at dark. But it was dull going.

Then on the third night the wind changed and started blowing from the east. It howled and wailed through the pines and you could feel the chill in it. We shivered and dug deeper into our sleeping bags.

In the morning it grew still colder and mist flew off the falls in clouds.

"We'll do better now," said my guide, Edgar Eastman.

That morning we took a couple of 8-pounders, a 9-pounder, and five grilse from 2 to 4 pounds. We went in at mid-afternoon for dinner so we could be out for the evening fishing.

It was getting colder by the minute. The mist swirled low over the pool and blew heavy from the falls. Before we went out we put on extra woolen shirts and our heaviest coats. It was almost cold enough to see your breath.

As we pulled up towards the falls, I wiggled into my bow seat and pulled my coat tighter about me.

"It's blowing off the ice," said Edgar.

He meant the ice in Greenland, and the bergs in White Bay, only 25 miles away. I shook a little harder while he poled the canoe up into the pool. He dropped the rock, let the line out, and then, sure of his position, made the line fast. We were

A grilse and a salmon from Newfoundland's famous Humber River.

anchored now about 50 feet above the drop off in probably the best spot in the pool. Anything could happen here.

I turned and looked at the 12-foot wall of water above us, stretching from one side of the river to the other. As I looked, a couple of grilse leaped into the face of it, four-foot tries, and then a bigger fish shot up, a 15-pounder, quivering all over. He almost made it. He fell short of the top by two feet.

It was a thrilling sight, the salmon busting up into the face of that tremendous fall of water, through it, head on, and into the rocks beyond, falling back, bruised and banged, and going up for another try. This was it, the greatest salmon pool in the world, and the salmon was the greatest fish. I squared away to cast.

Then Edgar almost scared me out of my wits.

"Can you hear them?" he whispered right in my ear, as he crouched in mid-canoe.

"Hear what?" I asked.

"Shh!" he said. "The rocks! They're tumbling! Hear them!"

I listened, and sure enough, faintly, I could hear a rumbling, like rocks rolling against one another, down there, deep.

"When the rocks tumble," said Edgar, "That's when the salmon hit. The big ones."

"Look out," I said. "I'm casting."

I dropped a size 8, low-water green highlander 15 feet out to the right. A six-pound grilse met it before it had floated a foot. I landed him. Ten minutes later I took a four-pounder. Then I had a terrific fight with a ten-pound fish that jumped and threw the hook.

Suddenly, "Look!" said Edgar.

I had seen it, too. In a slick spot between two rocks, right where the water poured over the tail of the pool, a great salmon came up in a head and tail rise. He looked as long as a canoe paddle. This was the one the tumbling rocks had promised.

I dropped the fly six feet above where he had showed, just in case he had moved upstream when he rose. Then I lengthened each successive cast a foot. Wherever he was, I wanted that fly to cover him, and in the right way. I mended the line, led the fly down with the tip of the rod guiding the floating line. I was using the greased line method of salmon fishing, the way of showing the fly broadside to the salmon, so he'd take on the first rise. I kept a slack line so I wouldn't get excited and strike too soon. I knew that if he took, and I gave slack, the current would belly the line downstream and pull the fly into the corner of his mouth.

Then I made the cast that would go over the spot where he had showed. I held my breath. He took, and I was into him.

From a standing start, that fish went to 40 per. He ran 20 feet and then I saw the line coming up and I got ready for the jump. He broke through in a terrific leap, five feet up, four feet forward. He looked like the butt end of a 30-year-old birch tree.

"Forty pounds!" I yelled.

"He's a dreadful fish!" said Edgar. "Play him easy."

I was too busy to answer. That fish rushed past us, headed for the falls. I turned with him and the blast of the east wind blowing off those icebergs slammed into my face, but I was too excited to feel the cold.

The salmon rushed on, reel click going in high.

"He's going to jump the falls!" shouted Edgar. "Watch him!"

I was watching him, all right, but I could no more have stopped that run than held back a steamroller with a willow twig.

He came out, straight up into the face of the falls for nine feet, hung there for a second, then fell back into the water. Seconds later he was jumping ten feet below us. I reeled fast, trying for a tight line, but he was on his way back to the falls again.

Once more the blast of cold air hit my face, and then he came out for five feet this time, as if just taking a look-see, and then veered off to the right.

"He's making for the fish ladder," said Edgar.

That salmon was heading for the right side of the falls, where steps had been blasted out a couple of years before. He made a jump up into it, then we saw his back as he hopped over the second step.

"Look at him!" I yelled. "Look at him! He's going home!"

"Home is right," said Edgar, seconds later, as the fly shot back in our faces.

I reeled in the vacant line and leader, wiped the spray from my face, and a few tears, and tested the 6-pound test tippet for fraying. It was in bad shape, so I tied on another and put on a size 8, low-water green highlander.

I cast it out.

A grilse hit it hard, bounced out and threw the fly a mile. I was 9:45 and almost dark. I reeled in.

"Let's go, Edgar." I said. "Let's go in and boil up."

Because, right then, no other salmon would do.

Twenty years from now, I thought, as we ran the rapids homeward, I'll be sitting by a campfire and saying: "That time on the Humber was terrific. The wind was blowing from the east, off the icebergs. And a mammouth salmon hit my green highlander and ran the Great Falls."

"It was a shame to lose him," said Edgar as we toiled up the hill to camp.

That night I dreamed about a big, husky salmon that swam up to me, touched me on the shoulder with a fin, and said, "Thanks for letting me go."

"Letting you go!" I said back to the 40-pounder. "You had me groggy from the start. All I did was hang on."

"Well anyway," said the salmon, "I've thanked you."

And the last I saw of him was his great, silvery body, like the butt end of a thirty-year-old birch tree, jumping over the falls with yards to spare.

8. *Those Freedom-Loving Sickletails*

The permit of southern waters is fast, powerful and shrewd, and he doesn't want publicity. That's why the all-tackle record has never exceeded a mere 42 pounds, 4 ounces.

"PERMIT!" shouted Captain Floyd Majors.

Fred Pabst, Jr., of Manchester, Vermont, cast the blue crab two feet in front of the black, sickle-shaped caudal fin the guide had sighted. He held his breath as he waited, then saw the entire tail as the feeding fish stood on his head to suck in the bait. He waited to be sure that the fish had it deep, then, as the tail slipped under and line started to go through his fingers, he braced and struck. The spinning reel shook to the core as the hook went home and that permit bolted and shot down the shoreline.

"He's a big one!" cried Floyd Majors. "You'll never stop him. I'm going to crank up and follow."

"Make it fast," gasped Fred. "He's taking line by the handful."

The outboard buzzed into action and they took off after the charging fish, Fred reeling desperately, trying to get line back, and Majors just as busy dodging jutting coral rock in the shallow water.

"He's running as fast as we are!" cried Fred. "And I can't give him any more butt on account of the line."

"You and your five-pound test," groaned Majors.

Then with a snort of relief, he gunned the motor as at last the skiff cleared the shallows. The fish was running steadily

91

down the shore. A mile and a half from where he hit, he turned toward the Gulf Stream. The chase moved seaward perhaps another mile and a half, only to reverse itself when the permit turned back, quartering a bit, toward where the fight had begun.

He had weakened some, now, from the long, hard pull, and Fred was putting line back on the reel. On the flat again, at Craig Key where they had started, Majors killed the motor. But somehow that permit didn't seem so tired. He circled, using his big, flat body broadside to the boat. He was good at in-fighting.

"He's pulling my arms right out at the shoulders," moaned Fred.

"Pump him," said the captain.

"Pump!" replied Fred. "What do you think I'm doing? This fish is killing me."

But bit by bit he was gaining in that tug of war and at last he steered the permit alongside and Majors netted the fish, which weighed an even 36 pounds and was posted by the International Game Fish Association as the world record permit caught on line testing under 12 pounds.

Found throughout the Caribbean area and up the Florida coast, with a few strays going further north in the Gulf Stream, the permit is strictly a warm water fish. They are seen in tempting numbers from Miami southward, and farther down the Keys that are fairly numerous, particularly at remote Content, Harbor, Sawyer and Johnson Key on the outer fringes as you look to the Gulf of Mexico. Still further out, they frequent exotic places with euphonious names like the Marquesas and the Dry Tortugas Islands, favorite permit spots, where the angler really has a chance because there are usually enough permit that he may muff a few casts and still try again.

At Content is perhaps the hottest permit fishing of the entire Keys. There you see great schools flittering along over the white sandy bottom in unbelievably clear water, a perfect mark but a hard target to hit.

They feed on the shallow banks sometimes, in water from 12 inches to six or seven feet deep. Schools numbering from a few to 20 fish move smartly along in military formation, snatching food as they go. When they flash suddenly into a sandy spot, their dorsal and caudal fins are waving black streamers, marking their course. No bottom-feeding fish moves faster.

As is the case with every species that anglers seek, fishermen tell stories of monstrous permit seen, but the biggest one on the books of the IGFA is the all-tackle world-record catch made as recently as Sept. 11, 1953, when R. H. Martin took a 42 pound 4 ouncer while fishing at Boca Grande, Florida. Only report of a larger member of the species taken on rod and reel was a 62-pound fish sent to Al Pflueger from Bimini in the Bahamas 20 years ago for mounting. But that tremendous catch apparently went unheralded among anglers generally. Anyone catching a 62-pound permit today would be famous.

The old saying that there are bigger fish in the ocean than ever were caught certainly applies to the permit. Dixie and Bill Knowles, well-known Keys guides, found that out first hand as they fished the reefs off Tavernier. They were commercially fishing for muttonfish and grouper in 60 feet of water and were using handlines that tested 72-pounds, strong enough to pull down a B-49. Their sturdy 8/o hooks were baited with crawfish. Dixie had a strike, and feeling perfectly secure with that stout line, heaved back and started hauling. Imagine his surprise when the haul went into reverse and he found the line slipping through his heavily gloved hands. He braced his feet and tugged back and fifteen minutes later hauled over the side a permit that they both knew was no teenager.

Hardly had that one flopped aboard when something almost yanked Bill out of the boat. He tightened, and yelled as 200 yards of line zipped out. Finally he stopped the run and the fight was on. That fish gave Bill a fit. It ran and sounded and tore things wide open until he despaired of ever landing it. Neither fisherman could guess what it was until, 25 minutes after the strike, Bill raised it to the surface and they saw that

he, too, had connected with a big permit. By the time he had
that one in the boat his calloused hands had deep grooves in
them, his gloves hung on by shreds and his fingers were sore
and bleeding. It was a bigger fish than the one Dixie had landed.

When they reached shore and weighed those permit, they
went 45 pounds 4 ounces, and 48 pounds 8 ounces, both heavier
by far than the existing IGFA world record.

While it may only be due to the fact that more anglers fish
the Keys than cover other waters where the permit is found,
it does seem that big permit like that area. A quick survey of
IGAF records bears this out. Two of the listed world records
were established on the Keys—E. J. Arnold's 41 pounder, a
20 pound test record; and the womans' all-tackle record, 38
pounds; both taken at Islamorada.

Yet while the above are world records, reports continue to
pour in about great hulks of permit roaming far waters and
scaring the pants off timid anglers. I talked to a native of the
Isle of Pines, Cuba, and he told me about catching 80-pound
permit on handlines off the south coast of the island. He claimed
to have seen some that would weigh 100 pounds. At Bimini,
an anglerette guided by Captain John Cass tied into a permit
that weighed 42 pounds. But just before it was landed, the
line wrapped around the tip of the rod and broke it, thus
spoiling the unhappy lady's chance at both the men's and
women's all-tackle record of the time.

Light-tackle angling for permit has only come to the front
during the past few years. Before that a scattered few went
for them with the lighter thread lines and with plug and fly
casting outfits. In 1950 Bob MacChristian of Miami cast a
spinning lure in front of a feeding permit, had a hit and an
hour later boated a 23-pounder, an outstanding catch on 5-
pound line. That, as far as can be learned, was the first record
of a permit caught on an artificial lure cast and retrieved in
regulation spinning manner on regulation spinning gear. (Fred
Pabst set his world record with a spinning outfit, but used bait.)

But since that time many other casters have taken permit on small, lead jigs on 1/0 hooks.

There are also a number of reports of permit being taken by plug casters. Miamian, Howard Clark, leads the field with two, a 26½-pound fish caught in 1949 and a 31¾ pounder taken in 1950. He took both at the same spot, plug casting from Long Key Bridge on the famed Overseas Highway to Key West.

With suitable modesty, the author claims the only two permit ever recorded as taken on fly-fishing equipment, one 5 pounds 10½ ounces, and another that went 11 pounds 8 ounces. Both were taken at Content Key.

From the moment of my first encounter with him, the shy and elusive permit has been the fish I dream about. They may not be too numerous and they are difficult to get to, but they put a fever in a fisherman's blood.

Permit are bottom feeders, the majority of the items on their diet being found on, and in some cases under, the ocean floor. Even those who are familiar with the rising blood pressure occasioned by the discovery of a bonefish tail sticking straight out of the water, admit that there is extra punch to the sight of the black sickle of the permit cutting up into the air, disappearing, and slashing up again 10 feet further along his course. They feed fast, darting along peering into holes in the coral, looking under rocks, digging into grassy beds for tasty shrimps and crabs, and, as they feed, head down, their bodies tilt upward and in shallow water their tails break the surface and flash in the sunlight. The sight of a permit tailing is one of angling's greatest thrills. It does things to the knees.

The flat-bodied permit is designed for the tough, flashy life he leads, with a framework of ribs that can take a terrific pounding. I have seen the little gaff topsail pompano and the common pompano feed in the surf on sand fleas in the midst of tumbling breakers that knocked them to the sandy bottom and slammed them on the beach. And recognizing the similarity of the permit in form and feeding habits, one would naturally expect them to have stout ribs. But my first view of a

The author with a 19 pound 15 ounce permit taken on a fly.

permit rib was an eye opener. Taken from a 22-pound permit, that rib, just below where it joined the backbone, was 2 inches across and almost an inch thick. The composition was as hard and dense as ivory. There are four ribs of this nature, then they taper rapidly towards the tail, where the ribs are again mere fish bones.

Permit have a habit of sunning themselves, lying on the surface with the tips of their dorsal and caudal fins sticking out, head down, dozing it seems. In such a position they look as if they were on the flats feeding and tailing, but they must either be asleep or very intent on scanning the bottom because when they behave in that manner it is possible to get much closer without frightening them. While I have never had a hit from one at such a time, once at Content Key when we were fishing for baby tarpon in 10 feet of water I watched a more or less accidental encounter with one. We were into tarpon up to our ears. I cast to what I thought was one of that species and had a hit but didn't connect. Then Bill Smith, my companion, yelled he had a permit on. It put a permanent screech in Bill's reel and the hook pulled out when he had run 200 yards in 9½ seconds flat. After that we looked more closely when we went for baby tarpon and sure enough, we began to find permit feeding and staying right with them as they moved along.

For three years I had the good fortune to be one of a party that took off on a sort of busman's holiday every spring. The personnel was made up of several well-known Keys guides—Captains Bill and Bonnie Smith, Captain Leo Johnson and his mate Steve, my wife and myself, with transportation supplied by Captain Leo's charter boat the *Islamorada*. The jaunt was strictly "Operation Permit" with equipment limited to fly tackle, and with only occasional sorties for snapper for the table. Our first trip will always be a sad memory of endless, fruitless casting to hundreds of permit. School after school swept by without even a side glance at our offerings. Now and then a single would deign to follow a fly for a few feet, then fade away. Day after day we cried in our coffee and figured ways to make a permit take a fly. We knew they could be taken on feathers, trolling, because it had been done. They should hit a fly.

On the last afternoon of that first trip, I finally had a hit. He took a white streamer fly and departed with both fly and leader. I'll never know whether the leader was not attached to the fly line properly, or if the line had been rubbed across some coral rock till it had become weakened. I do know that that was, and still remains, the blackest spot in my fishing memories.

The next year we went back loaded for bear with every kind of fly, feather, spoon and lure that could be cast with a fly rod. This trip we had three hits and I landed a 5 pound 10½ ounce permit that hit a Johnson Golden Minnow Spoon, fly rod size. Things seemed better, but even then, being purists all, we did not feel that we had really proved a permit would take a fly.

Meantime, we heard reports of this and that angler tangling with a permit on fly equipment—how so-and-so almost landed one that hit a yellow bucktail or a red and white streamer. Dick Splaine of Key West had had several hits from permit and Hagen Sands of Islamorada had tangled with four that were bigger than average. The first, and largest, Sands estimated at 50 pounds and this baby hit and started for Europe and never did stop. He took everything Sands had in the line department, whisking it from the reel a mile a minute, the fly line, 200 yards of backing—then, zing! exit Mr. Permit. Three others around the 30 pound class, put up terrific fights, one of them taking Sands a mile out to sea before breaking off. Another got away in a hurry, and the fourth supplied the real heartbreak. Sands had his hand on the fish when it gave a last desperate wiggle and snapped the leader.

But in spite of our own past grief and that of others we knew, we set out on our third annual trip last spring more pepped up than ever. This was going to be the payoff.

The first day out it blew 20 miles an hour and things were plenty tough for fly casting. The wind even blew our retrieved line out of the bottom of the skiff and finally Bill Smith and I, who were partners that day, decided that we should go overboard and wade the flats. We pushed along, about 30 feet apart, peering at the bottom for the shadowy forms and scanning the surface for the sickle-shaped tails. Suddenly I saw Bill stop and cast directly upwind. The fly dropped and the dorsal of a permit cut the water as the fish went for it. There was a big swirl as he took. And then, as Bill struck, that permit made a comet seem slow. He went across the flat so fast he seemed to knock the waves down in front of him, like a bowler making a strike in every frame.

I turned and looked at Bill. His face was all happiness.

Then he came back to earth. "He's taking me!" he yelled. "My backing is nearly gone!"

"Maybe he'll turn!" I yelled back.

"He's going too fast for that!" Bill cried.

A minute later I saw the rod tip bend down almost to the water then spring back up. The line jumped back, too. The fish had run the line out to the reel core and then snapped the tippet.

Later that same day, Leo had his share of being pushed around by a permit. One fish hit his fly so hard that it knocked the rod right out of his hand. It fell into the water and as he groped for it with his right hand, he forgot that he still kept a grip on the line with his left hand. That galloping ghost went out of there like chain lightning, and almost cut his fingers off before he snapped the leader tippet.

"Why, that little round-nosed rascal!" said Leo. "Look what he did to me."

The next day Bonnie Smith dropped a fly right in the teeth of a school of tailing fish and three of them bumped pectorals as they rushed for it. She put home the steel and held the rod high as a 20-pounder reached out for Brownsville, Texas, and never stopped. If he kept his course and his speed, he made the 900 miles in 36 hours. But perhaps he found a patch of sand somewhere out in the Gulf of Mexico, and just rubbed that fly out and forgot about it. Bonnie was still shaking an hour later.

The same day, my wife, the only other feminine member of the party, also joined the ranks of those who have hooked and lost permit on a fly. With Bill poling her, she spotted a tailing fish in deep water. She cast the fly, felt the fish and set the hook. He had just got warmed up in a 100-yard dash, a mere trial run, when the fly dropped out of his mouth.

The last day, Bonnie and I went out together and I started

right off with a strike from a fish that fought like a 40-pounder. While I had him on, I could see Bill overboard, casting and chasing after a fast-moving school that had come in on a particularly nice bit of sand beach. He hooked one and suddenly I saw it slant over toward where mine was making like a bucking bronco.

"Get that minnow out of here!" I shouted. "He'll cut off my permit."

"Minnow!" screamed Bill. "It's a 30-pound permit. Look out or he'll sink you."

Then both fish got off within seconds and Bill and I glared at each other across the barren water as if each had caused the other's misfortune.

"Well, anyway, that's eight permit we've had hit flies this trip," I said to Bonnie when my temperature had gone back to normal. "At least I feel sure now that they'll make a fly rod fish."

"Well, don't waste your time talking about it," she said shortly. "Get a fly to one of that school over there and we'll be back in business."

Sure enough, there came a school of probably 50 fish, showing black above the light bottom. As we watched, several of them turned sideways, their silvery bodies signalling like a battery of heliographs.

"Try one of those three!" Bonnie said tensely, and I saw where three were swimming along, single file, coming our way. "Cast and pray," she added.

I dropped the fly in front of the first one. The prayer came double from both of us. "Take it. Take it. Take it." I muttered in time with the strip of my retrieve.

And he didn't hesitate, just moved forward a little faster, slanting upward, opened his mouth and swallowed that fly. I struck.

That permit went out of there faster than the reel could click, as if every porpoise in the ocean were after him. He made a straight-away dash then curved to the left in a looping run that made the line slash through the water. And he held that wild curve till my backing was almost gone. He had close to 700 feet of line out. I was going through mental convulsions trying to hold onto that backing just by wishing. And then, just as if the wishing worked, he turned and came charging at us, a mile a minute, so that he got ahead of the line and I had to reel and reel like mad to try to keep up with him. A couple of times he had so much slack that it seemed to me he could have reached up a fin and pushed that fly right out of his mouth. That was when I began to call him mine. I knew he was thoroughly hooked.

I finally got the line tight between us again. And he was slowing. But it was just to try a new trick. He flipped his tail and rubbed his round little nose in the sand till the rod shook and so did I. No matter how firmly that hook was in there, those were tough tactics. Desperately I pulled harder and turned him completely over. That hurt him and he staggered some, while I kept horsing him as hard as I dared on the 8-pound test nylon leader. Then he got his nose down and rocked the rod tip again until I thought he would pull the top section off. I held on with both hands. If anyone ever wanted a fish, I wanted that one.

Once more he headed straight out, still showing plenty of power. But this run was a mere hundred feet and then he went into a series of short dashes, off tackle to the right, then reversed his field and slashed back the other way.

"He's tiring," said Bonnie. "Stick with him."

"Uh," was all I could reply.

He came close in then and I turned him over as he tried to rub his nose again. I kept him coming, with rod held high and managed to lift him away from the bottom as he circled the skiff once, twice, three times. Standing on the seat, then, I turned to Bonnie.

"Ready?" I asked.

"Uh—yes." she answered in a small voice. "I have no landing net but—"

"No net!" I cried in anguish.

"We forgot it," she stated in a firmer tone. "So I'll just pick him out of the water by his tail. That's why permits have those handle-shaped tails, you know."

Silently I swung him around, Bonnie kneeled in the bottom of the skiff, arms out over the water. I pulled the tired fish in, raising him to the surface. Bonnie reached out as if she landed permit by the tail any old day. She groped, her body between me and the permit. There was a splash and I closed my eyes.

"You can look now," she said calmly. "Here he is."

She was holding a shiny, silvery permit on the bottom of the skiff. He weighed 11 pounds 8 ounces.

Editor's note—since this story was written the author has landed a 19 pound 8 ounce permit while fly fishing at the Isle of Pines, Cuba, with Captain Vic Barothy. Three other permit have also been taken on flies by other anglers.

9. Add A Little Salt

When a brook trout goes to sea, he returns to his native waters fat and sassy and full of fight. The scene is laid in Newfoundland.

MY GUIDE, Edgar Eastman, and I walked down to the sea. We passed several of the best salmon pools on the Serpentine River without stopping. We'd heard that the sea run brook trout were bunched at the mouth of the river waiting for high water to start their upstream run. And I wanted to catch one of those brookies in the salt.

We reached the tidewater pool and went on down to where the river emptied into the ocean through high-piled gravel bars, a narrow outlet that a good broad-jumper could cover in one hop.

The sea was calm, and evidently the tide was making in because where the river flowed out, foot high waves piled up as the two currents bucked each other. If there were any hungry brookies around, that was where they would be.

I tied a red and white bucktail to my 4-pound test tippet, a good-sized fly dressed on a No. 4 hook, and I edged in to about 40 feet from the moving water and made my first cast into the sea for a brook trout. It dropped two feet the other side of the current and I brought it back in slow, foot-long jerks, working the rod tip to give the fly action.

Then there was a swirl at the fly, and as I tensed I saw a flash of silver. I felt a thudding shock that numbed my fingers on the rod grip; my left hand, stripping line, was yanked forward.

Then the rod tip dipped down almost to the water and the reel started clicking, slowly, then faster, then a steady scream.

"I've got him!" I yelled.

"You bet," said Edgar.

That fish ran 60 feet in six seconds, a dizzy dash down the river current toward the open sea. Then he veered to the left, across current, and over there he got broadside to me and sat back and pulled. I pulled too, but I couldn't budge him. He began to shake his head so hard that I had to give him slack by dropping the rod tip. Then I raised it again, gingerly, and he was still there. He was moving up-current now, toward the river mouth, slowly, so that I could reel line in and still have it tight. But he didn't like fighting that current, so he turned and waltzed down the shoreline.

"How big do you think he is?" I asked Edgar.

"Maybe four pounds," he said. "A nice sea trout."

"It can't be a brookie," I said. "They don't fight as hard as this fish. Whatever, he is, he's seven or eight pounds."

I got him turned at last and kept him coming. But he still had other tricks. He started rolling in the leader, and that was tough to handle, but eventually it was that very trick that did him in because he got the leader twisted around his gills so that he couldn't fight.

He was a beautiful fish, a brookie for sure, and about four pounds, just as Edgar had said. But in this sea-going version, the characteristic bright reds and oranges of the brookie were overlaid with a skim of silver so that the markings hardly showed.

"A lot more silver than I expected," I said.

"It takes about a month in the fresh water, and then you can't tell whether or not he's ever been to sea," said Edgar. "By that time, he's as bright as a maple leaf."

These sea-run fish are the eastern brook trout, *salvelinus fontinalis*, the native of the east, the same fish that is called speckled trout, squaretail, and brook trout on the mainland. The mud trout of Newfoundland is the same fish, too, deriving its uncomplimentary name from its habit of lying over mud in ponds and backwaters of rivers.

Their original habitat was the eastern seaboard of the United States from Georgia through Canada, and as far west as Manitoba and Michigan, but free-handed stocking has taken them to many parts of the world. In 1947, while fishing the tidewater pool of an unnamed river along the Inland Passage of Alaska, I hooked into one of these transposed easterners far from his home grounds, but as fat and saucy as they come. Here, too, as in coastal streams from New England to Newfoundland, some of the brook trout leave the rivers and go to sea, and whenever they do so, they give an account of themselves on their return that is considerably better than the fight made by those of the species that stay in their native fresh water.

The first brook trout to stick his nose into the sea must have been a venturesome fish. Probably pickings were lean that year and he was hungry. The river was almost devoid of all the things he had formerly lived and grown fat upon. The nymphs he used to dig out of the pebbles and stones on the bottom, and the naturals he took from the surface, and the minnows he used to chase and catch in the shallows—all were few and far between. So he had worked his way down to the tidewater pool, and found better forage. But he didn't like the feel of the salt on his gill rakers, so he quickly beat it back to the pure water of the pool above. But hunger got the better of him and he returned to the tidewater pool again, and for a week he kept nosing into the salt, getting used to it, finding more food than he had ever seen.

Several times he retreated to the pool above, to taste again the sweet water there. But each time that hunger drove him down he became more accustomed to the sea water and began to swim further out in the bay. And one day, he moved along with the outgoing tide and slipped down the shore until he was ten miles away from the river mouth, a full-fledged sailor, quite at home in the salty seas, feeding on smelt and capelin, growing fat and strong.

Anglers return to town with sea run brook trout caught near Gambo. Newfoundland, in the Gambo River.

It was hunger that took him down to the sea in the first place, but an even more compelling urge eventually brought him back. A month and a half after he first went into the ocean, something stirred in him, insistently, the urge to spawn. And he started back to the river where he was born.

Again he tarried at the tidewater pool, going in and out of the tide, this time getting used to the fresh water. Then, with a goodly high tide he made the bore into the river and headed up. He was "fontinalis," a fish of the springs, and that was what he was looking for, springs or seepage that would maintain a constant temperature as protection for the eggs that would be deposited on the gravel beds away up in the smaller parts of the river.

And the continuance of his species attended to, he would winter over, and with the spring, with the breakup of the ice, he would head down again and out to sea in quest of the great abundance of food there.

In the old days, Newfoundlanders used to take trout by the barrel during the winter season, and one old timer told me that the fish were so hungry during this period that they would take any bait from a piece of red flannel on up.

"But rabbit's tongue was best," he stated. "It was red and tough and we could catch half a dozen on one tongue."

To protect the fish during their winter stay in the ponds, lakes and rivers, and during their run to the sea in the early spring, it is now legal to take sea run trout from May 24th to September 15th only. The daily limit is 24 fish, except in the Serpentine, Fox Island, Castors and Western Brook, where due to the enormous size of the fish, the legal creel limit is 8 sea run brookies per day.

The runs that really provide the fishing come into the rivers in late July and early August, and the fish come in successive waves, usually in schools of about the same weight, ranging from little fellows five and six inches long, to giants of the species, some of them reaching twelve pounds. Fish eight and nine inches long carry roe or milt and are capable of reproducing their kind.

Once at South Brook, with Fisheries Warden Art Butts, I watched six-inch brookies leap up the face of a two-foot high falls.

"They're full of spawn, too," said Art. "Even those tiny fish. They're on the way up, just like the big fellows."

I cast and caught one of them, just to look at him. A sheen of silver overlay the brookie markings, proof that he had been to sea. He was firm and fat and strong, as befitted a little fish that was performing an amazing journey, ten miles or more upstream through rapids and over falls. I put him back, knowing that with good luck, one day this little beauty might give someone a sporting battle, when he was three or four pounds, or more.

While the west coast rivers of Newfoundland have the reputation of holding the largest sea run brook trout, at South Brook and around Gambo anglers bring in an occasional big one as well as the two pounders which are general there. Rocky Schulstad of Grand Falls took a 5¼-pounder at South Brook last summer, and several of that size were brought in at Gambo, as well as one 11-pound fish.

Rocky ties a number of flies especially for sea-runs, and one in particular is worth describing. I call it the "Traverse Brook Sea Trout Fly" because that's where I first saw Rocky using it. The dressing is as follows:

Tail—yellow, golden pheasant

Tag—silver oval tinsel

Hackle—red, palmered along length of body

Body—claret floss

Wing—caribou hair (light)

Head—black

Generally speaking, in the early season the red-bodied flies or streamers, dressed on large hooks, sizes 4, 6 and 8, pay off. Then in the late summer, small flies dressed on size 10 and 12 hooks are in order and even as small a fly as a size 16 will do business. Practically any of the trout patterns used in United States and Canadian waters will take sea run brookies. The Silver Doctor, Parmachene Belle, Cow Dung, Black Zulu, Terra Nova (silver body), Jenny Lind, Dark Montreal, Bumble Bee, Marlodge, Royal Coachman, Gray Hackle, Brown Hackle, Professor and Quill Gordon, in sizes 10, 12 and 14, all produce, as do the various streamers and bucktails that are in common usage for the stay-put members of the brookie family.

The red and white, black and white, all black and all white bucktails are sure fire, and the muddler is away up in front as a strike bringer. The black, white and yellow marabous are excellent flies, and the Grey Ghost and Royal Coachman streamers all produce plenty of strikes.

The best dry flies for Newfoundland sea runs are the Royal, the Brown, the Gray and the Grizzly Wulff patterns, and the hard to beat old reliables, the Gray Hackle and the Brown Hackle. The bivisibles do well, with the Black and the Brown taking top billing, as also do the hair-bodied dry flies in grey, grizzly and black. Dry flies should be dressed on size 12 to 8 hooks.

The ideal fly rod for sea run brookies in rivers is an 8-footer, weighing 4 to 4½ ounces, and fitted with an HDH nylon fly line and a 14-foot leader tapered down from a 25-pound test top section to a 3-pound test tippet. Such tapering makes the leader easier to cast and prevents the line from slapping down near the fish. In this sea run fishing, as in all trout fishing, a finer leader and lighter presentation will bring more strikes.

The reel should be large enough to hold 100 yards of 10- or 12-pound test nylon squidding line for backing, as well as the fly line. You never know when you might tie into a big one and have to follow him downstream; or, fishing for brookies where you do, you might hang a salmon at any time.

For bigger water, and for the salt, and along the beaches, an 8½-foot fly rod, weighing 4½ to 5 ounces, with a matching HCH fly line, is needed. The same backing mentioned above will serve on this outfit, but in the heavier water it is advisable to end the leader with a 4-pound test tippet.

The last time I was in Newfoundland, as I was sitting at the lunch counter in the airlines terminal; a tall young fellow in Pan American World Airways uniform came up and introduced himself.

"I'm Cal Osmond," he said. "What are you here for? Atlantic salmon, I suppose."

"Partly," I said. "But also sea run brookies. Ever fish for them?"

"Do I! I was brought up on them."

Cal remembers catching them when he was a kid, at Bluff Head near Gambo, about five miles from Traverse Brook. And he and a lot of fellow members of the Gander Rod and Gun Club know the answers still, on the salt water brookies.

"This summer I went back there, and it was just like old

"Boiling up" to make tea is part of the Newfoundland fishing scene. Note the typical Newfoundland kettle.

days," he said. "They still hit best on high tide and at dusk. I caught them from half a pound up to 3½ pounds."

At Bulley's Cove, about eight miles from Point Leamington River, near Botwood, he found sea trout that walloped his streamers and fought like they had been training for just that occasion. Those two-pounders didn't know when to quit. And at Campbelltown Estuary, Cal discovered the top spot in a summer of good fishing. There, he waded out into the salt and tied on a Norsklure, a famous Norwegian salmon fly that he had found to be sure death to Newfoundland brookies—a fine representation of the capelin, a six-inch-long, smelt-like bait fish found in the shallows around the island. It has tandem hooks, the front a number 2 and the one at the rear a number 10, and it is dressed with olive green wings and a silver body. In the water it looks alive.

That was a dish-calm day and Cal could see fish working, see the waves they made as they swam slowly along just under the surface. He dropped his first cast three feet in front of a "wave" and started a series of foot-long strips. The wave speeded up and hit the fly with a thump.

That trout knew all the tricks and tried them all, but Cal beat him down and brought him in, a fine three-pounder. That afternoon he landed nine that went from 2½ to 3½ pounds, all on that Norsklure that looked so much like a capelin. The two fish he kept to eat each had a single capelin in the stomach.

Undoubtedly the capelin is the mainstay of both the sea-run trout and the salmon in these waters, and "Capelin For Sale" signs that appear in front of every Newfoundland grocery store are as good a forecast as any that the sea runs are in the bays. At Hall's Bay I saw the surface riffled by thousands of capelin coming to the shallows to spawn. They swam in circles, working, spawning and dying. We could see the dead ones lying belly up on the bottom while countless others swam over them to deposit their milt and roe and so join the silent ones in the bottom. Local people were dipping them up in buckets, to be fried and eaten like smelts.

But while it's top fun to catch brookies in the bays and estuaries, and at the mouths of the rivers, there's something about moving water and the woods around that belongs to brook trout. And when you find them there, in the river where they belong, but strong and hale and just returned from a trip to the sea, that's an extra dividend.

The year after I had fished the mouth of the Serpentine with Edgar Eastman, I went back there again with Jim Young of Flat Bay doing the guiding. This is one of the rivers where the runs come in wave after wave, 2-, 3-, and 4-pounders, and some that go 5 and 6—not many, but enough to provide great angling—and in back of all those assorted sizes come the chiefs of the clan, great 10- and 12-pounders, huge slabs of fish-flesh, almost impossible to believe.

When we reached the Dump Pool on the first morning, I had hardly gotten my rod rigged up before I heard a shout from Jim.

"Quick!" he shouted. "Look at this."

He pointed to a great dark spot showing on the bottom. It extended half way across the pool and well down towards the tail.

"Those are big sea trout," he said. "Thousands of them."

I took off the low-water Jock Scott I had just tied on my leader and got out a size 10 Royal Wulff.

"I'm going below them," I said, "and show them this dry. If they are going to hit at all, they should hit this."

We walked well back from the pool, and eased in below. I dropped the fly on the outer edge of the dark spot and a fish rocketed up and took just like that.

He flipped over and dove right into the middle of those closely-packed sea run brook trout and a great hole appeared for a moment, then closed in again. My fish was already across the pool, taking line. Then he did a complete circle of the pool as if it was a racetrack, a sea-strong trout with the bit in his teeth. Then, well below me, he surfaced and began shaking his head. I gave him slack and ran down his way because I know the three pound test tippet couldn't take too much of that in such fast water. At last I got a tight line on him again and then when I put the pressure on, he began to tire. When we finally netted him, he was a nice three pounds.

We went back to the pool and on my third cast another trout roared up and grabbed the fly; and he, too, dashed into that bunch on the bottom. They scattered, and this time stayed scattered. They didn't like being the target for those dive bombers.

When I landed that one, it was a 3-pounder, too. "Probably a school of 3-pound fish," I said.

"There could be some bigger ones there, too," Jim told me.

A little later as I was about to pick up the fly, a big, wide mouth clamped down on it. I didn't have time to set the hook —he took so fast—and before I knew it he was half-way up the pool, and flying.

"That one's seven pounds!" shouted Jim.

"The big one you said could be there," I grinned.

Then that racing trout turned on a dime and came back our way. And somewhere along the line the hook dropped out of his mouth. He didn't even show to wave goodbye.

For consolation, I took five more from that pool, all three pounds, and one that hit three and a half. That kind of fishing makes you forget losing a seven pounder—almost.

10. Boca Fever

In a few hours I caught the two biggest trout of my career. Yet the Argentine fishermen hardly rated them as keepers!

WE CAME over the hilltop and there was the lake, and the river pouring out of it.

"The boca!" shouted Jorge Donovan.

"The boca! The boca!" yelled Bebe Anchorena and Andrew Gordon.

All three were Argentines who knew their country's rivers well. If they could become so excited about their first trip of the season in the foothills of the Andes Mountains, then what they'd been telling me must be true. This was the place where the spotted monsters lived.

We were working out of Junin de los Andes, a small town on the eastern slope of the Andes. You can reach Junin, in Neuquen Territory, by plane and car. From New York or Miami to Buenos Aires it is less than a day's flight by Pan American World Airways. From Buenos Aires you go by car across the great Argentine pampas in two days. Or you can fly from Buenos Aires to Bariloche, then drive a rented car 150 miles over good gravel roads. Plane fare from New York to Buenos Aires is around $900 round trip; cars can be rented for $12 a day in Argentina. A plane flight from Buenos Aires to Bariloche costs little—less than air transportation in the United States. And the rate of exchange heavily favors the

American dollar. When I fished there last winter—their summer
—one American dollar got me 28 Argentine pesos.

Unlike many South American fishing waters, the rivers
in the Junin area lie at a comfortable 2,500-foot altitude.
They're the world's greatest trout streams, most of them
seldom fished. In a month I saw fewer than a dozen anglers. I'd
drive fifty miles along great, trouty rivers and not meet one.

These rivers flow out of vast lakes containing enormous
trout. Thirty- and 35-pound fish are taken by the few trollers
who venture out on these lakes, but boats are few and the water
usually too rough for comfort. But the rivers—the Chimehuin,
the Alumine, the Collon Cura, the Quilquihue, the Quillen, and
the Malleo—are jam-packed with 4-, 5- and 6-pound browns
and rainbows. These aren't considered keepers, and a 9-pounder
is just part of the day's catch. A competent angler can be sure
of a 10-pounder and, now and again, a 12-, 15- or maybe 20-
pounder. Tiring of that, you can drive, in three hours, to the
Traful and the Limay, two of the greatest landlocked salmon
rivers in the world.

The choicest spot on a river is the boca, the first pool just
below the lake from which the river runs. "Boca" means mouth,
and in the Argentine foot-hills the place where the water pours
out of a lake to form a river is called a boca—Boca Lolog, Boca
Chimehuin, and so on. Big fish? The word "lunker" must have
been coined by a fellow fresh from a boca.

"This is the Boca Lolog," said Jorge that first day. "The
water is so clear that you'll be glad the wind is putting a riffle
on it."

Riffle? Three-foot-high waves were rolling in and the wind
was blowing the tops off them!

"There are some fish in the bocas all summer—that is, in
January, February and March," Jorge continued. "But I'll
take March as the best month for the biggest fish. That's
when they're getting ready to drop downstream to spawn."

That sounded strange. I'm accustomed to fish that run upstream to spawn. But there are few large feeder streams

The 18½ pounder that fought for three quarters of an hour before being landed. He hit a fly rod popping bug.

above Argentine lakes into which a trout can run, so they go
down into the broader rivers. Still it seemed strange that they
should reverse the usual direction of run, since these trout are
descendents of fish brought from other parts of the world and
planted in Neuquen Territory lakes in 1903. Lake trout and
whitefish were also planted, but have disappeared. The landlocked salmon, browns and rainbows thrived.

When the browns and rainbows first leave the lakes for the
bocas, they are a bright silver, like fresh-run Atlantic salmon.
They are firm and sleek and pack the wallop of a Firpo.
That's because they dine well on two-inch-wide greenish crabs
that look like heavy, clawed editions of our crawfish. The lakes
and rivers are loaded with them. The fish also take natural
flies, nymphs and minnows about 1½ inches long, called
puyen.

"Let's go," said Bebe. "You start right here, Joe."

I stepped into the water. It was cold. I moved out, and a
big wave slopped water all over my right side. I eased my way
to within casting range of the channel, got a good firm grip
on the gravel bottom with my felt soled waders and looked
the situation over. This could be the home of big trout all right.
Water was sliding out of Lake Lolog through a 250-foot-wide
exit to form the Quilquihue River.

I got line out and shot the big 4-inch red-and-yellow
streamer fly out for sixty-five feet. I started it back in foot-
long jerks—just two of them. There was a terrific swirl under
the streamer. Startled, I struck prematurely. The high-riding
fly left the water and shot my way. I stripped in line and
waited, giving that trout time to get back to his feeding
station. When I cast again, he let the fly come halfway back,
then hit it so hard that he almost jerked the 9-foot fly rod
from my hand. He headed downriver for four hundred feet,
then came out in a startling end-over-end jump. He was pure
silver, a big rainbow.

He jumped again, as high as a kite, swapped ends, sizzled off
on another 150-foot run, greyhounded, came back my way,

changed his mind, went downstream, came out in a straight-up try for the sky and threw the hook.

I'd never before been tied to a rainbow that big. He must have been nine pounds. I was numb all over, and it took me a long time to reel in the line.

Ten minutes later I saw another fish slashing at my fly. I kept up the slow, steady retrieve. He socked it and ran up past me, headed for the lake. Then he jumped clear, and as certainly as the other had been the biggest rainbow I'd ever had on, this was the biggest brownie. He looked to be ten pounds.

He lit and kept on for the lake, but after a hundred feet I turned him. This time he ran downstream, and kept going until he was a couple of hundred feet below. Then he came halfway out, sank back in and kept boring off, taking line slowly from the reel.

I couldn't hold him, so I started walking after him, keeping the line tight but not able to gain any back. I eased into the shallower water, reeling fast, ran down his way for a hundred feet, stopped and reeled some more. Then I lay back on the rod. He was a hard-mouthed, big-jawed bull of a brownie, but I finally turned him and headed him my way. At last I saw the leader come out. I kept skidding him shoreward until he was out of the water and lay still. Reaching down, I put a handfull of fingers into his gills, carried him ashore and weighed him. He went 9¼ pounds.

As is usual when fishing is good in the Andes foothills, clouds were low. A misty rain had started driving at my back; my right side, where the water had splashed me, was like ice. I tightened up my collar and turned back to the business at hand. A few casts later I saw a big brown shape in back of my fly. He hit like a triphammer, stuck his snout out and began shaking it until I thought the rod would come apart. But I dropped the tip fast and he drifted downstream, then got a finhold and tore off as though someone were jabbing him with a pitchfork.

He ran for 130 feet, stopped and shook his massive head again. I went after him. He ran some more. So did I. He gained on me, and I got stuck. There was a deep hole in front of me, and I had to walk fifty feet toward shore to get around it. Luckily he'd found another hole further down and was resting in it. I went on down, reeling fast, and got opposite him. I got him moving again, going downstream slowly; so I knew he was tired. I tightened the drag. He was too big to play with, too big for gentle handling. You can't baby a bosco like that one. You have to play him boldly, or he'll get off. I put a bend in the rod, and the pressure finally got him. When I skidded him up on the gravel beach, I wished I hadn't kept that little 9¼-pounder. This one weighed 10¼.

I sat down and mopped my feverish brow. In a distance of little more than a hundred feet and in less than an hour and a half, I had landed the two best trout I'd ever caught. No one back home was going to believe me. And in the next half hour I took two more nice rainbows, a 5-pounder and a 7½-pounder.

You only have to see a few fish like that and hear about a few more to get boca fever for fair. Last year a spoon fisherman on the Chimehuin Boca came up with a 21-pound brown. In the Boca Lolog another spoon angler took a hook-jawed brownie that weighed 26½ pounds. A couple of years ago, still another spoon fancier, in one day, took a 20-pound brown trout, two of 15½ pounds, two rainbows and two browns of 13 pounds, three rainbows and two browns each running 11 pounds, and one 6½ pound rainbow. Fishing like that doesn't happen every day, or even every year! But those big ones are there, and this fact makes any angler's temperature jump.

It's said that the Limay Boca, head of the great Limay River, has the biggest rainbows in all Argentina. Thirty- and 35-pound rainbows have been caught by trollers in Lago Nahuel Huapi, the lake that feeds the Limay, and those big fish sometimes move into the boca. This is one of the few bocas where skiffs are used, and from them you can see the fish through

The husky 11 pound brown trout that took Brooks 300 feet downstream in the Boca Lolog.

the crystal-clear water, great hulks that every now and then rise up and shine as they bust for the heavens.

In all the Argentine bocas I fished, big flies proved much better than smaller ones. The big fish scorned small stuff. After the first day on Boca Lolog we seldom used anything smaller than a 4-inch-ling fly tied on at least a number 2 hook. We even used larger streamers, some with wings five inches long and tied on a 1/0 hook. The bigger the fly, the bigger the fish seemed to be. They wanted bulk. And while occasionally a big fish is taken on a small fly, browns and rainbows of 9 pounds and up seldom hit a fly smaller than four inches. Best colors are red-and-yellow, blue-and-white, brown-and-white, red-and-white, all yellow and all white.

The next day, on the Boca Chimehuin, Bebe took a 10-pound rainbow; Jorge, an 8½-pound brown and a 7-pound rainbow.

Andrew took a 6-pounder of each. I landed a 7-pound brown and a pair of beautiful rainbows that went 7 and 8½ pounds.

A couple of nights we camped, while fishing the more distant rivers, but otherwise we stayed at the Hosteria Chimehuin, our headquarters. The hosteria is a Waltonian's dream of heaven on earth. Everything is geared to the fisherman's life. The first thing you hear in the morning is the clump of waders as some early riser rushes to the nearby river at dawn. During the siesta hours of midafternoon when the fish aren't hitting, the spacious lawns are littered with socks spread out to dry and fly lines coiled loosely on the grass or stretched between trees, sharing the sun with strings of trout fillets from the morning catch. The dried fillets are later smoked, bottled and carried home for off-season snacks.

Unlike many resorts, food is served at the hosteria at the angler's convenience, not the cook's. In the gin-clear water of Andean streams, fish do not hit during the bright part of the day, from one until six o'clock; so most anglers fish in the morning, come in for dinner in the middle of the day, have a siesta, rise at four for tea (another full-fledged meal) then wend their way streamward for the evening fishing. Anglers often stay out until eleven; so the evening meal may be served at midnight.

The Boca Lolog was wonderful, but the Chimehuin became my favorite. This pool was eighty feet across and two hundred feet long. Waves bounced into it from the lake, but on the five-foot-deep channel there was only a riffle. The wind that roars into that boca, like a blast from the polar regions, all but blows you over.

"When it's from the north," Jorge told me, "it's wrong. Then it's blowing up river and into the lake. You never catch fish on that wind."

"But we only get north winds about three or four times a season," said Andrew. "Most of the time it's a west wind, and that's the best wind for the bocas. It's west today."

It was west, right enough, and cold, pushing up three-foot

waves that doused us. Over the lake, huge billowing black clouds reached up high. Below them other clouds blotted out the mountains. We could see water pouring out of them.

"We're going to get it good," I remarked.

"Not necessarily," said Andrew. "Those storms seem to hang over the lake. Most of the time they never reach the river."

He was right. We felt the dampness of the storm, but it stayed up on the lake. Where I was fishing, the wind was coming at an angle, and I really had to put the rod to it to make any kind of throw. But with that 9-foot glass rod and GAF line I managed to put the streamer out about 50 feet, to a spot where the water poured past a rock. As I started it back, a wave hit me and almost knocked me flat. I kept the fly coming, picked it up and cast again. For twenty minutes I fished without moving from that spot, and I didn't have a hit or a follow that I could see. Yet I had a hunch there was a big fish near that rock. I showed it everything I had. No luck. Then I looked deep in my tackle bag and came up with a 5-inch fly-rod popper, a devil to throw in the wind, but just the right medicine for a big trout. I tied it on, wound up and put it out there. I started it back slowly and then saw a great shape in back of it, a long brown form that appeared from nowhere and put its nose on that moving bug and followed after it. I stripped again, slowly, so as not to make it pop and maybe scare that thing away. I stripped again—the shadow followed.

Sweat burst out on my brow and suddenly I was cold all over. Should I stop stripping, increase the speed or pop the bug? I decided to stick to the retrieve that had got him interested. I kept stripping and hoping. Then that fish came down on the popper with a thump that jolted me so hard that my feet slipped from under me and I fell sideways into the fast current. I was loaded with clothing; if I ever got caught in there, I'd never get out again. So I made an all-out effort and scrambled back to my feet.

Ardent fly rodders all, this group of Buenos Aires anglers are off to the Boca to try for the big ones.

Then I became conscious of a singing reel and realized that I was still clutching the rod in my right hand. The fly line was all gone and the backing was leaping from the whirling reel. Below me the bottom shelved up; so I scrambled down, got into ankle-deep water, and chased that fish. He went out of the tail of the pool into water that dropped off to 15-foot depth, and kept right on. Traveling like a bat riding a gale, he went through the second pool for 150 feet, then came into the air. Even at that distance, he looked like a horse!

He kept boring away, taking line again. I had to go down the shoreline after him. But I kept reeling and put the pressure on. It took twenty minutes more to get him in close, and then he half-rolled in the shallows and I thought I'd lose him after all. But I held the line tight and somehow managed to keep the leader clear of sharp rocks. I skidded him into inch-deep water, reached down and grabbed him through the gills.

Until then I hadn't known there was anyone else around. But a crowd had gathered. Jorge, Bebe and Andrew were there, and Don Jose Julian, proprietor of the hosteria, came hurrying up with scales.

"Fifteen pounds," he announced.

I was shaking so hard that my teeth were rattling.

"What's the matter?" asked Jorge. "Are you cold?"

"Boca fever," Bebe laughed. "He's got boca fever."

I knew it was true and that I'd never again be really content until I got back to fish these fabulous bocas again.

But the time had come to go, and after dinner that night I went to pay my tab. I found Don Jose apologetic.

"There has been a slight rise in price," he said. "When you first arrived, the charge was $1.40 a day for everything. But then it went up to $1.50. However," he added, "after the rise in price, all wine was free."

It happens that I do not drink wine. But I still contend that ten cents a day was a small premium to pay for Utopia.

11. The Hat Trick

**When clouds put a topper on Lanin, a volcanic
Argentine peak, the fishing becomes "fantastico."**

I OPENED MY EYES and looked out of the
car window at a perfectly formed peak sticking up into the
sky, its top covered with snow and ice. We were in the foothills, and if I hadn't known otherwise, it could have been
Colorado, Wyoming, or Montana. The desert-like vegetation
of the Argentine pampas, through which we had been driving
when I fell asleep, had changed to a thick, yellow-topped
thorn. And there was lots of sagebrush.

During the night we had rolled along in a cloud of dust, the
headlights now and then picking out a short-eared Patagonian
hare, or the black-masked vizcacha that looks like a cross between a raccoon and a possum. Now, just at dawn, we flushed
a Patagonian rhea, a variety of ostrich. With its ungainly three-
foot-long neck held high, it went dashing over the slope above
the road.

"They're smaller than the African ostrich," said Bebe. "The
gauchos eat the eggs. Wings, too."

We saw a group of the wild-looking gauchos by the road-
side soon after that. They sat comfortably on their sturdy
horses, saddles padded with cojincillos of soft sheepskin. They
were almost completely covered with ponchos made of vicuna
wool. A gaucho can practically live under his poncho and
keep warm even in coldest weather.

Each of these picturesque Argentine cowboys carried his

127

Looking downstream on the Chimehuin River-country very similar to Montana, Wyoming and parts of Colorado.

bola wrapped around his waist. It consists of three woven thongs, each ending in a skin-covered lead ball. Holding one ball in his hand, a gaucho can whirl the other two balls around his head, and toss the bola at terrific speed. It will entangle a steer's legs and drop him. Bola-throwing gauchos are just as expert at snagging an ostrich.

Jorge, who was driving, looked back. "There's Lanin," he said.

"That mountain?" I asked.

He nodded. "You'll be looking at it a lot during the next two weeks. That mountain range in the distance is the Cordillera de los Andes It runs all the way from Panama clear down to the tip of Tierra del Fuego. Some of those peaks are more than 20,000 feet high, but the Lanin, which is the important one to us, is lower, about 12,500."

"Why is the Lanin so important?" I asked. "Is it a volcano?"

"An extinct one," he said. "But see that little cloud sitting right on the top, like a hat? When Lanin has his hat on, the wind will blow, and fishing will be good."

"No hat, no hits," said Bebe. "Today he has his hat on."

"It's because the rivers are so clear," Jorge continued. "You can see the pebbles on the bottom at 20 feet. So the best fishing is when it's windy, cloudy, or even raining. When it's bright you may as well take a siesta. The fish just won't hit then."

I looked at the Lanin and hoped he'd keep that hat on. But at the same time I had mental reservations about staying in siesta even on the brightest afternoon, not after travelling 6,000 miles to fish for the big Argentine trout Jorge had told me were here.

I had met Jorge Donovan in a tackle store in New York, and like all fishermen we started comparing notes. My home is in Florida, and I told Jorge about taking bonefish on flies. Within a week we met in Florida, and in a couple of days he'd landed a 7½-pounder and an 8-pounder.

"Wonderful!" he said. "But now you must come to Argentina and I will show you big browns and rainbows that will break you up. In some of the lakes, trolling, they get 30-pounders. But we'll stick to the rivers, because that's what we both like, and you'll get the biggest trout you ever caught."

And that's how it came about that I hopped a Pan American World Airways plane in Miami one day in January, and the next day was driving west from Buenos Aires with Jorge Donovan and his friend, Bebe Anchorena, two of Argentina's most enthusiastic fly fishermen. We were headed for the eastern slope of the Andes, where the rivers pour down to the plains from mighty, snow-fed lakes.

As we neared the Junin de los Andes, where we were to stay, we saw some Araucano Indians plodding behind wooden plows pulled by oxen. On the mountain slopes forests of Coihue trees rose as high as 100 feet. I was told that some of them were five feet through at the butt.

It was late afternoon when we reached the Hosteria Chimehuin on the outskirts of Junin de los Andes. It didn't take us long to whip into our fishing clothes, grab our gear and hightail it for the Chimehuin River. There was a good wind blowing when we stopped by the Elbow Pool.

"This is where you start," said Jorge. "There are 8- and 10-pounders in here."

I tied a four-inch-long streamer, a red and yellow combination, on my leader.

"What's that?" asked Bebe. "A feather duster?"

"You said big fish," I said. "And big fish like a big mouthful. Try one."

I handed each of them a similar fly. They looked sceptical but pocketed them and took off downstream.

I waded out to cast, starting with a short line that I lengthened a couple of feet each time until I was throwing about 60 feet. I cast across current and brought the streamer back in slow, foot-long jerks. Each time I'd strip, the feathers closed in on the hook. When I stopped, they flared outward. It made the fly look alive.

I made half a dozen casts. Then I spotted a long, dark shape behind the fly. With dorsal fin clear out of the water, that fish fell on the fly like an avalanche. He left for the tail of the pool so fast that I thought he'd pop his scales. He made the water smoke for 150 feet, then came out in a broadside, going away jump. He splashed back in and headed for some rocks on the far shore. He must have nicked the leader or run it across a sharp rock, because the fly line snapped back at me, minus the big streamer.

I just stood there for a minute. My first strike in this river, and I'd lost a 10-pounder!

I looked up at the Lanin. He had his hat on, sure enough. I tipped mine. "You know your business," I said to him.

A flock of bandurrias came flying my way from across the river. They were big, ibis-like birds, with long, decurved bills, and they greeted me with a series of startled honks that sounded like a bunch of kids blowing ten cent horns. They zoomed over the bank in back of me, flighting in to roost.

It was 8:30. I had another hour before dark, so I tied on another big streamer. On the third cast I had a hit that I felt through my fingers, up my arms, and down to my toenails.

This fish was dynamite. He rushed my way. Then he turned and I struck again, just in case the hook had loosened. That made him mad for fair, and what he'd done before was peanuts. For the next 10 minutes I was withstanding a series of explosions. Then he sulked deep in the current, letting the water hold him there. He was so quiet I began to wonder if he'd wrapped the line around something, or had lodged the hook in a log and left me holding the stream bottom.

I banged the rod with the butt of my hand. That sent shocks down to him and he began to move, slowly at first, then with increasing speed. He didn't like those jolts. I saw the line come up, fast, and he jumped a foot above the surface, looking like a slab of molded bronze. His spots looked as big as saucers.

Ten minutes later I skidded him up on the shore, jumped on him and got a good grip on his gills. Then I rushed him away from the river. I was taking no chances on a wild flop.

I was just putting him on the scales when Jorge walked up. "Nine and a half pounds," I said.

"Mine weighs only seven," said Jorge.

He held up a beautiful seven-pound rainbow he'd had in his hand all the time.

"Get any others?" I asked.

"I put back a couple of six-pound brownies," he answered.

On our way back to the car a bunch of teros gave us a fit. These birds, like the bandurrias, seemed to object to fishermen. They kept yapping at us with shrill, rasping sounds, circling round our heads in a storm of raucous noises. Crows, magpies, jays and other loud-mouthed birds are pikers compared to teros, whose vocal cords must be made of metal.

Bebe showed up at the car with a 7½ pound rainbow. It

was beautiful, sleek and silvery, and had given Bebe a terrific battle.

Next morning we had good fishing weather again, which means it was raining. By the time we got to the river the rain had turned to mist, just enough to keep our faces wet. The fish were rising.

I started using dry flies in my pool. They kept me busy for three hours—rainbows and browns from 3 to 6 pounds, and a top fish that went 6¾. In all, I must have hooked 30 fish in that short time. At noon, Jorge and Bebe came back.

"Seven pounds," said Bebe, holding up a brownie. "He took a streamer."

"An 8-pound rainbow," said Jorge, showing his fish. "On a big streamer, too."

"A 6¾-pound brownie," I announced, and added by way of apology, "but he took a dry, and on a 2-x tippet."

"We'll go back to the hosteria for lunch and a siesta," they told me.

"I'll take the lunch," I said, "but I don't have any plans for a siesta."

Jorge looked at the sky. The clouds were gone, a bright sun beat down.

"There won't be any fishing until at least 6 p.m." he said.

I didn't argue, but as soon as they had gone off for their siesta, I headed back to the river. Three days later I'd had enough of siesta-time fishing to convince me that Jorge was right. Those fish wouldn't hit when the sun was shining smack on the pools. It had to be cloudy, windy, or rainy, except for early morning or evening. But when conditions are right, the Chimehuin stacks up against any trout stream in the world.

The Chimehuin (pronounced chim-e-wee-an) flows out of Lake Huechulaufquen (which-u-lof-kin), winds 22 miles down the mountains to the picturesque little town of Junin de los Andes, and finally, after being swelled by two other feeder streams, joins the Colloncura 18 miles below. The entire river lies at a comfortable fishing altitude of about 2500

The ·Hosteria Chimehuin at Junin de los Andes, always filled with anglers throughout Argentina's summer season, from January to April.

feet, and all 40 miles of it is loaded with trout. Any pool may have a 12-pounder, maybe one weighing 15 or 20 pounds. In a single day, a fair angler can count on landing several fish in the 7- to 10-pound bracket—and he'll probably lose flies and leaders to a couple larger ones.

It's a big river, with pools over 100 feet across and 600 to 700 feet long. But in most places it's easy to wade, with a gradual slope toward the deep water. Like·all rivers, the fish often seem to lie on the far side. A long cast pays off.

While many trout are caught daily on spinning and bait-casting equipment, fly tackle takes more fish because of the lighter presentation of the lure in the extremely clear water. A big streamer or bucktail fished on a fine leader will catch more lunkers than anything else.

All the standard fly patterns in use in the United States—both wet and dry—do well in Argentine waters. Since it's difficult to buy flies in Argentina, you should go armed with a complete supply. The only tyer I encountered was Jose Navas, manager of the Norysur Club on Lake Meliquina. His Matona ,a streamer, is one of the best to be had, and his nymphs are also real producers.

Most Argentine anglers use Atlantic salmon flies and standard wets. They catch fish with them, too, but the lunker trout, the real heavyweights, seem to prefer something like a five-inch-long bucktail or streamer.

Partly to handle the big flies, but mostly because of the constant wind, it's best to have a nine-foot fly rod and a matching GAF fly line. On some of the smaller streams, and for dry fly fishing on all the rivers, we used 8½-foot rods with GBF lines. But you'll ordinarily make a lot of roll casts and change-of-direction casts, and be bringing your rod tip down almost to the water to get your flies out in or under the wind. And that's when the bigger rod pays off. It doesn't always blow a gale down there. Perhaps for an hour or two, or even a day or two, you may fish in comparative calm, but I leaned back against the wind for so long that a couple of times I nearly fell backward into the river when there was a sudden lull. Yet it has to blow a lot harder than that to stop a trout fisherman. You soon learn to buy a Basque hat, which stays on, and to thank the wind for producing more strikes.

We had two weeks of unbelievable fishing. We fished the Chimehuin from one end to the other, using everything in our fly boxes—weighted nymphs, hairbodied dry flies, streamers, bucktails with five-inch wings. The fish liked most of what they saw. It was a slow day when there were no 8-pounders. Four- and 5-pounders were routine. The fishing was, as the Argentines say, "fantastico."

One afternoon just before dark I was fishing Elbow Pool when Bebe came rushing up my way. "Give me another of those big flies," he gasped.

I handed him a streamer. He grabbed it and rushed away before I could get out a word. After he disappeared around the bend, I decided I'd better wander down and see what was going on.

Bebe was fishing the pool above the rapids known as Garganta del Diablo, the Devil's Throat. He was casting a long line, retrieving the fly, casting again. You could tell from his actions that he was expecting a hit from a lunker. Then out in midstream something socked his fly and threw up a screen of water that just about blotted out the far shore.

Bebe's line jumped back his way. He examined the fly, muttered to himself, and started casting again. Nothing happened. A few more casts and it was too dark to see. Bebe waded ashore and walked up to me.

"He must have been 25 pounds," he said. "Fantastico!"

It started to snow on the way home that night and it got plenty cold. Fresh from Florida, I was shaking up a fit. I put my sleeping bag over two thick woolen blankets already on my bed. It was February 10, but that's the middle of the Argentine summer, like our August 10. Nevertheless, when I looked out the window the next morning, snow was all over the foothills and the high mountains were packed solid.

We couldn't see the Lanin to get a fishing forecast, as it was still cloudy and spitting snow.

"It will be a good day," said Jorge.

That day each of us took some 6- and 7-pounders and Jorge crashed through with a fine 9¼-pound brownie that liked the looks of a red-and-white streamer. Then, as if by magic, the clouds rolled back and showed a bright blue sky. Business was over until after the siesta period.

About 5 p.m. I was watching Jorge fish the boca. Right away he hooked a rainbow that looked to be 12 or 14 pounds. It smashed the pool into a thousand drops of water. It belly-whopped and jackknifed. It walked on its tail and stood on its head. It was a wildcat on fins. Then it showed us how fast a rainbow can run. For 200 feet it flashed through the water, then came up with another leap. The fish slowed then, and Jorge started following it downstream, reeling just fast enough to keep on a heavy pressure. He walked faster, got in his backing and some fly line. Then he strained on the rod, turned the fish, and got him coming.

That "tired" rainbow shot toward us, went past a mile a minute, and 20 feet beyond us jumped again, head over caudal, his crimson sides a blaze of glory. But he tired fast after that, and Jorge led him gingerly across the shallows and slid him up on shore. He weighed an even 10 pounds.

After congratulations, I hurried off to start in a pool of my own. I passed Bebe in the Elbow Pool.

"I left the Garganta Pool for you," he said. "It should be good tonight."

As I waded in I looked at the Lanin. He had his hat pulled down over his ears. I made a cast. I had a hit, landed a 6-pounder and released it. I got a 4-pounder and put that back. Both browns. I moved further down.

It was tough casting here because of a high bank in back of me. The pool was 125 feet across where I stood. Seventy feet below me it spilled into the Garganta del Diablo, a quarter of a mile of rocks, boulders, and white water. Any hooked fish that reached that raceway was a goner.

Right in front of me the current slipped along at a neat clip, with only a couple of feet of wadable water before the bottom dropped off abruptly to a six-foot depth. A trout, I reasoned, would lie in front of that protruding rock out there on the rim, or between it and the shore. And right here the shore became a rocky ledge that shouldered right into the water. A great flow of current swept along that ledge and then busted into the white water of the rapids.

"It's a hopeless place to play a trout," I thought. (But it was a perfect lie for a big trout.) "Big fish like a big mouthful." I mumbled to myself as I searched through my fly box. A guy needed something like a five-inch bucktail, a streamer, or what have you? And suddenly I saw it—a what have you. It was a big gray popping bug with yellow deer-hair tail. I tied it on my 6 pound test tippet, tried the knot and was ready.

"Here's your big mouthful," I said. "Come and get it."

I tossed the backcast high over some bushes behind me and made the forward throw, shooting the line at the same time. The big fly-rod bug hit 60 feet straight out. I let it float quietly, without imparting motion, until it began to swim in toward my bank. Then I stripped in slow, foot-long pulls making bubbles with the bug, but not pops. I wanted to attract trout but not scare them. Nothing happened.

I stripped five more feet of line off the reel and shot the bug out again. This time I jiggled it slightly as it floated. Before it started to swing my way I began to strip, bringing it fast across the tail of the pool, past the protruding rock, along the lip and in toward the ledge. I let it hang a moment directly below me, then started it upstream, without pops, with just a slight gurgle.

Suddenly, a great, wide-open mouth engulfed the bug, and the upper half of the mouth snapped down. As I struck I saw the head and shoulders of a great trout. I felt his strength for a moment; then he dived and I couldn't feel him at all. The line was tight, but there was no movement. I was sure he'd run me around a rock or a log at the submerged base of the cliff.

I began reeling fast as I walked down that way, keeping a tight line, taking no chances. I reached the ledge and my line went straight down. I could see the top of the 12 foot leader. I could also see a black cave under that ledge, about four feet down. If the fish was still on, he was in there. It looked hopeless.

"Well, here goes," I thought, and stuck the nine-foot fly rod as far out over the water as I could, away from that cave. "Maybe I can pull him out."

But I didn't have to. That trout shot out and up, clearing the surface not ten feet in front of me. He looked to be 25 pounds.

I almost fell in. One foot slipped down the drop-off and I pawed madly for a foothold. But automatically I held the rod high and survived the monster's jump.

He sulked then and gave me time to think. My only chance

At dark, Bebe Anchorena came in with a 13½ pound brownie that had hit a large white bucktail, the "platinum blonde." Looking on, left to right, Lou Klewer, Outdoor Editor of the *Toledo Blade;* Col. Larden of Buenos Aires; the cab driver Jose Julian; proprietor of the Hosteria Chimehuin; and Bebe's daughter, Carolina.

was to get him away from the boiling rapids of the Garganta run below me. I pulled back on the rod and began inching my way upstream. I walked him up for 100 feet, like a bull on a nose ring; and then, just as I was beginning to breathe again, he came halfway out and shook his head at me. His teeth looked as long as a crocodile's. He almost scared me. Brownies just don't come that big.

He liked it on top and kept thrashing around on the surface. He rocked the rod and threw buckets of water. When I dropped the tip to keep him from snagging the leader with his teeth, he took advantage of me and dashed downstream for the rapids. He didn't stop until he was right on the brink of the pool, and then I guess he stopped only because he didn't like the look of the rapids any better than I did.

I walked down to the cliff again and started all over. This time I worked him up 200 feet. I put more pressure on then and he came to the top. He peeped out at me and left on a faster run than the first, headed for the other shore. When he slowed, I turned his head upstream and his dorsal fin came out.

Then he began to give me the creeps. A hundred feet across the current and about 50 feet down, he began boring away from me with wide flaps of his tail. It was an Atlantic salmon trick, a wicked, line-swatting thing, and I had to admit it was a good move from the fish's point of view. I ran downstream, reeling fast, until I was opposite him, then I pulled hard on the rod and got him turned my way. He charged across and jumped not 20 feet out from me, mouth wide open, showing all his teeth. That leap gained him 35 feet of line and gave me 35 more gray hairs.

Once again he wound up on the lip of the pool and once again I went down and started him back. I was still afraid of those rapids. Even if he tired, I couldn't hold his dead weight out in the fast water with the tippet I had on. So I edged him upstream. Inch by inch, I walked him as far as I could, about 250 feet above the tail of the pool. There the tree limbs came down to the water so thick that I couldn't get under them, and the drop-off was so sudden that I couldn't wade around them. This was it. This was where I'd have to make my play. I pulled him my way, found that he was almost ready. He could make only a feeble flap now with his big, broad tail. I pulled some more and he came to the top and rolled over on his side. He was as long as my leg.

But now I had another worry. I had no gaff, no net, and the bank jutted up too high to beach him. I'd have to tire him completely and pick him out of the water.

He righted himself and started boring away again with slow flaps of his tail. Each beat might pull the hook out. It was brutal. I pulled the rod in toward my bank, held him for a second, then turned his head and reeled the leader halfway in through the guides to get him close enough to reach. But he turned and threw water all over me as he dashed for the deep.

I stopped him fast, this time, and pulled him on his side against a rock. As he lay there quietly, I slipped my fiingers through his gills, lifted him, and ran up the bank. Halfway up he gave a convulsive flap with his great body and almost pulled me over backward. But I had a death grip on him and I kept going until I hit the path.

Then, at last confident that he couldn't kick himself back into the river, I laid him down and with shaking hands got out my scales. He weighed 18½ pounds. He was an inch short of being a yard long and had a girth of 22 inches. It had taken me three-quarters of an hour to land him.

I grabbed him up again, popping bug still in his mouth, and ran up the path toward the pool above, where I knew Bebe was fishing. I rounded some bushes and there he was, working upstream with a dry fly, his back to me.

I was so excited I wanted to shout, but I went quietly to within 15 feet of him. Then I shed my jacket and sat down on the bank, braced myself, and held up that great trout.

"Look, Bebe!" I proclaimed. "Una marone grande!"

12. Outlandish Trout

Anglers and sheep need extra layers of wool in the world's southernmost trout country. Fishing, however, is red-hot.

I STOOD in the river and shivered. I remembered that the Fuegian Indians of long ago went fishing with fires built on a heap of gravel in their dugout canoes, and now I knew why. It was cold, damp, and the wind had an icy cut, even though this was late January, which is midsummer on Tierra del Fuego.

Those Yahgans, the southernmost Indians in the world, had worn only little bits of otter skin. I wore heavy wool underwear, wool pants, two wool shirts, chest high waders over two pairs of wool socks, a fishing vest and a rain jacket. Around my neck was a long wool scarf that my host had forced on me before we left the estancia. I was grateful for it now, and I wished I'd thought to get some of those pocket hand-warmers before I left the United States.

Our first day on Tierra del Fuego had been typical weather. We took off from Bahia Blanca, Argentina, flew south for 12 hours over Patagonia and on across the Strait of Magellan to the southern tip of South America. Then we were over the Rio Grande airfield, and the pilot took a long run inland and made a circle over the small town below.

"That's the Estancia Maria Behety," said Jorge Donovan, my Argentine friend, who along with Bebe Anchorena; another Argentinian, made up our party.

141

The author pauses to sip mate, the national drink in Argentina. It has
much the quality of tea, and is brewed and served in small gourds and is
sipped through a silver straw.

"Which?" I asked, trying to single out what building he meant.

"The whole thing," Jorge explained. "The estancia is like a ranch. This one has 250,000 acres and 200,000 sheep. There are 159 people who work there; that's the reason it looks like a little town."

"They have their own machine shop, blacksmith shop, electric shop—even movies and a soccer field," said Bebe. "They have to be self-sufficient down here."

"The shearing sheds hold 7,000 sheep at one time," said Jorge. "And you never saw such thick wool. Because of the cold weather, I suppose."

I supposed so, too, having sampled the weather.

When we landed, the owner of the estancia, Charles Menendez Behety, and Duncan McKay, a Scotsman who has been his manager for 21 years, came across the field toward us, leaning into the wind. I held onto my hat as we shook hands.

"The truck is ready," said Charlie. "I knew you'd want to start fishing as soon as you could."

When we pulled up to the Rio Grande 20 minutes later I was grinning to myself. Fishermen are the same the world over. No group can move faster than a bunch of anglers getting to the fishing.

"Good luck," Charles called, as he left me in the first pool and went off to place the others farther downstream. "I'll pick you up at 11. Dinner is at 12."

I grinned again. He meant 12 midnight, for down here, only 700 miles from the Antarctic mainland, the summer days are 18 hours long.

The water was a little discolored, so I tied on a yellow streamer. Upon casting I immediately hooked a 2-pound rainbow that did most of his fighting in the air. And from then on I was busy with rainbows that went from 3 to 7 pounds, all beautifully colored, hard-hitting fish. It made me forget the cold . . . until I suddenly found that my fingers were too numb to grip the fly rod and my knees were chilled stiff.

The thrill of a lifetime! The author with his 18½ pound brownie.

That night at dinner Charlie told me that the three top fish of the previous year had been an 18-pound brown, a 16-pound rainbow, and a 16-pound sea trout, which is a sea-run brown trout.

"All on spoons," said Charlie. "On flies, the biggest were a 13-pound sea trout, a 10-pound brownie, and a 9-pound rainbow."

"I kept hoping for a sea-run brownie today," I said. "I've never caught one."

"They should have been in a week ago," Duncan McKay put in. "But we've had the worst winter in 50 years. Snow water is still coming down the river from the Andes, and we've had such steady rains that the rivers on Fuego are all up to bank height. If it rains again tonight, it will be too muddy to fish."

But the next day was clear and bright. Jorge topped the morning catch with a 7-pound brown, while Bebe brought in the best rainbow, a 6-pounder. We all threw back plenty of 3- and 4-pound fish.

We had instructions to meet at the Lone Tree Pool at 2 o'clock, as Duncan's wife, Christine, was preparing an asado for us. That's an outdoor barbecue, and in this case the meat was a whole lamb. Everyone gathered around, sharp knife in hand, and cut off his own strips of meat. We soon cleaned up every bit of that tender lamb.

"Leave this pool for me to fish, please," Christine said, when we finished. "I'll catch about six good fish for dinner tonight and take them back to the Estancia. Then you won't have to save any unless you want to."

"Such confidence!" I thought, as I headed down to the next pool. I saw Christine stow the last picnic package in the truck, take out her rod, and walk to the riverbank. She was using a plug rod with a big bronze spoon. On her first cast she hooked and landed a good-sized trout.

The next time I turned from my own fishing and looked around, maybe ten minutes later, I saw a sight I'll probably

never see again. In those few minutes Christine had landed five
fish, all in the 3- to 5-pound class. She hadn't bothered to kill
them as she brought them in, just dropped them on the bank
behind her, and there she stood, hooked to the sixth, while the
first five trout were still flipping and flopping.

Not much later I saw she wasn't the only one on that estancia
who knew how to fish. Downstream I came upon Carlos and
Alejandro, Charles' two young sons. They were sharing a pool,
standing 100 feet apart. As I watched, Carlos heaved his spoon
out and got a hit. He pulled that 3-pounder to the surface,
got a good grip on the rod handle while the trout jumped
and thrashed, and ran back from the river, pulling the fish
high on the shore.

Both boys were good casters, and aside from the tendency
to hang on, come what may, they put on an excellent per-
formance. Best of all, they put back every one of their fish
except the pair of heavyweights each of them carried when I
first saw them.

In the face of such fishing, it was amazing to learn that the
only fish native to Fuegian streams was a small perch. To obtain
fish at all, the Yahgan Indians had to look to the salt water.
When a whale was washed ashore, crowds gathered to feed on
it, no matter how putrid. The hazards of their seagoing ex-
peditions for fish are described in Lucas Bridges' book, *Utter-
most Part of the Earth*. Bridges, born on Tierra del Fuego,
spent much time with the Indians and learned their language,
which is varied and expressive. For instance, they have one
word for a man sitting in the bow of a canoe and a different
word for the same man if he's sitting amidships. Their word
for a poor man is "api tupan" which means "body only."

The Indians used to fish among the great kelp beds along
the shores of Tierra del Fuego, mooring their canoes to the
tough strands that came up from the depths. It was rough out
there, with 30-foot tides and great waves pounding in on the
clay cliffs.

An Englishman, John Goodall, who married a descendent

14-pound sea run brown trout caught on a streamer fly by the author, in the Rio Grande River on Tierra del Fuego.

of Lucas Bridges, was inspired to bring fresh-water fish to the island. In 1935, 1936 and 1937 he planted rainbows, browns, and brook trout in three rivers; and in the Rio Grande and the Ewan he also put landlocked salmon. These imports thrived phenomenally and, Goodall, who stall lived at Viamonte until his death in 1955, enjoyed many years of terrific fishing. The southernmost fishing club in the world is rightfully named for him, the John Goodall Fishing Club of Tierra del Fuego.

Goodall has taken browns, rainbows and sea-run brown trout resulting from his planting. For some reason the rainbows don't run to sea as they do along the Pacific Coast of North America. But some of the landlocks he planted in rivers seem to be going to sea and back just like Atlantic salmon.

These Fuegian trout hit a wide variety of local and North American flies. They hit standard wets such as the Coachman, Royal Coachman, Professor, Dark Montreal, Light Cahill, Black Gnat, Brown Hackle, and Gray Hackle in sizes from 12 to 8. They also took flat-bodied nymphs on No. 12 hooks, and the larger specimens fell all over big streamers and bucktails.

Bebe and I discovered that they also like dry flies. One day we saw a couple of risers just as we were starting to fish, and I quickly tied on a 4-pound test tippet, selected a No. 8 Royal Coachman hairwing dry fly, and put it over the nearest fish. He ignored it, but kept coming up.

I made a dozen futile tries before we saw a small natural floating past, a little black job. The rising fish fixed that baby in a hurry, so I added two feet of 2X leader as a tippet and knotted on a No. 14 Black Gnat. The fish took the first float and I set the hook.

He jumped, a long, bronze-hued brownie, much bigger than I had thought him to be. He kept racing for the other side of the river until he took all my fly line and was well down into the backing. He turned and ran upstream, then switched ends and went downstream again. Wherever he went, he didn't seem satisfied, leaving as soon as he got there. I finally skidded him up on a small sandspit and weighed him—a 6-pounder.

Two little boys with four big fish. Alejandro and Carlos Menendez Behety, have fishing like this right on their father's ranch on the Rio Grande River, Tierra del Fuego.

"That's the first fish I know of being caught on Tierra del Fuego on a dry," Bebe told me, but we went on to catch dozens that way. The best dry flies turned out to be Gray Wulff, Grizzly Wulff, the Royal Coachman hairwing, Brown Hackle, Light Cahill, and the Gray Hackle with yellow body.

It rained that night, and in the morning Charlie said we'd have to go upriver to get above the feeder streams that were pouring mud into the river.

As we drove upstream we saw a herd of guanaco. Closely allied to the llama, the guanaco was the prime source of meat and clothing wool for the Onas, the inland Indians on Tierra del Fuego. The Onas were once great bowmen and famed hunters; today there are only 20 members of the race still living (at the Estancia Viamonte, the home of the Bridges family) and the guanaco is little hunted either for skins or meat.

The herd we saw skimmed gracefully across the road in front of our truck, fleet as the wind. The male hung back, watching us till he figured the herd was safely away, then sped after them, the most effortless, graceful runner I have ever seen.

Later the same morning we saw kaikanes, the big geese that live on grass. They were another favorite food of the Indians and their down was used as tinder in lighting fires. But now no one eats them and they have multiplied until they are almost a nuisance.

This was a jackpot day for birds. We also saw two flocks of flamingos, totalling at least 200 birds. They were so pink they cast a glow on the water in their lagoon, and in the air around them. A little later we came on a pair of very rare sisne de cabeza negra, a huge white swan with jet-black throat and head. And just before I started to fish I saw my first steamer duck, a hefty waterfowl that may weigh more than 20 pounds.

When we got above the muddy water, we found the sea trout, too. Skinny Lalor and Luis O'Farrell, both of Buenos Aires, joined us that day and I was watching Luis spinning at the head of a pool. He had landed a 5-pound brown trout and then, just three casts later something grabbed his spoon and took off like a ball of fire. The fish ran 300 feet and scared Skinny out of his position at the tail of the pool, then shot back up and jumped 30 feet away from us. He had the gleam of freshly polished sterling.

"Sea trout!" yelled Luis.

That fish made another run through the pool and fought every inch of the way as Luis brought him back. Then, when he was in close, he took off a third time. That phenomenal strength must have come from his sojourn in the salt water because no river brownie ever fought that hard. But finally skill and tackle told, and Luis brought him to net. He was 6½ pounds, the first sea trout of the year on Tierra del Fuego.

Not many minutes later Luis took a 7-pounder. The sea trout were in, all right. Too late, I left Luis and headed off on my own—just as it began to rain so hard that even our tough crowd had to stop fishing. And since more rain meant more mud in the rivers, we felt glum.

"Nothing to do tomorrow but try the Ewan River," said Duncan McKay. "It's a smaller stream and the chances are that it will be clearer than the Rio Grande."

Next day we found the Ewan cloudy but clear enough that you could see a yellow streamer for a foot or two under the water. We got rainbows and browns from 2 to 6 pounds, but no searun trout. So next day back we went to the Rio Grande. Bebe had heard that a bunch of seals had been seen down where the river goes into the ocean. He thought they were following a run of sea trout upstream. The Rio was still not clear, but Jorge and Bebe were so sure that the sea trout would be in that we decided to fish it anyway.

It's a big river, many of the pools being 100 feet across and 500 feet long. When the water is high, as it was then, it's impossible to wade far out, which means you can't throw a big fly all the way across to the far bank. I cast for ten minutes and caught a 3-pound rainbow. Then, standing there in waist-deep water, I peered at the far bank and wished I could put the fly right against that shore. I was sure that if there was a big sea trout around, he'd like this streamer with its four-inch-long yellow wings, red hackle and yellow chenille body tied on a 1/0 hook.

Finally by really working at the double haul, I got a good 70 feet straight across current. I started the streamer back and was about to pick it up for the next cast when I saw a great swirl right under it and felt a walloping hit. Water flew as the fish socked that high-riding fly and headed for the ocean 10 miles downstream. He stripped 250 feet from my big reel and I began to worry. He took 100 feet more and I was sweating.

Shepherds dress in woolen ponchos against rain and cold, use sheepskin saddle pads. The sheep dogs are descendents of the original imports from Scotland, and are among the world's best working dogs.

I was caught flat-footed out in that deep water. Before I could make it to the shallows and run after him he'd have all my line.

"Let him go," yelled Jorge, who had suddenly appeared at my side.

"He's going to let me go," I growled, just as the fish slowed, stopped, and hopped high in the air.

"A sea trout!" Jorge yelled right in my ear.

faring fish was boring toward the thin water at the end of the

I was too busy to tell him I'd sensed that earlier. That sea-

pool and I was afraid he'd get into the rapids below. I began
to edge shoreward, but just then he turned back. I kept reeling
and kept the line tight. He came right in against that powerful
current until I got the fly line back on the reel. Then he headed
downstream again and took away everything I'd gained. Then
over and over with more of the same until we were both dead
tired. I put the rod to him and skidded him up on the sloping
shore.

He weighed 10 pounds, my first sea-run brown trout, a great,
silvery fish with the same black spots as a salmon. In fact, I
could hardly have distinguished him from either an Atlantic
salmon or a landlocked except that his body was thicker and
didn't taper near the stern.

Later in the afternoon, Jorge took a 9-pounder and another
that hit 5½ pounds. Then, as it was getting near dark, we
started for the car and met Bebe at the Lone Tree Pool.

"I've had some fair rainbows and browns up to 5 pounds,"
he told us. "But not the first sign of a sea trout."

He was disappointed, but still casting.

Bebe and Jorge are two of the best roll-casters I've seen.
Undoubtedly it comes from the amount of fishing they do on
windy Argentine rivers. A gale just doesn't faze them. They
pull their hats down tight, put the wind behind them, and roll
out 70 feet of GAF as if it were nothing.

That's what Bebe was doing now. He sent that big yellow
beadhead fly across current for 70 feet, then let it float downstream. It went 10 feet and stopped. Bebe lifted his rod, felt
nothing.

"Thought I had a hit," he called. "Maybe a little one grabbed
the tail feathers."

He got the fly in and made another beautiful roll to the
same spot. Again he let the fly drift free and again it went
10 feet and stopped. Bebe struck, fast, then shrugged. "Nada,"
he said. "Nothing."

Again he dropped the fly on the same place and let it drift.
This time the line stopped and Bebe's rod tip dipped. Some-

thing big was aboard, and it charged toward Bebe and came out in a leap right in front of him.

"Sea trout!" he hollered.

Jorge and I yelled, too, because it was a big one, and our shouts seemed to urge the fish on. It headed for the ocean far downstream. Bebe followed it at his wader-hobbled top speed.

Five hundred feet below us the sea trout jumped. It was a break for Bebe and he got some line back. Then he gained some more as the trout nosed into the current, getting its wind after that sensational dash.

Bebe put on the pressure and started the fish through a long series of runs and jumps. Bebe's steady pull kept the fish mad, bucking the heavy current and tired him fast. After a final flurry on the surface, Bebe pulled him up short, turned him completely over, and reeled him to the net. Then he waded ashore, his big grin wider than his face. His sea trout weighed an even 11 pounds.

"Am I lucky!" said Bebe. "The last cast of the trip and I get the biggest sea trout I've ever caught."

"I did almost as well," I said, holding up my 10-pounder. "My first and only sea trout."

"Me, too," said Jorge, lifting his 10½-pounder. "This is the biggest one I've ever taken."

"Think what we'd have done if the run had really be in," I said, because we were leaving for the mainland the next morning.

"Next year," said Jorge, "we'll hit the run right on the nose, eh, Joe?"

I hesitated. Tierra del Fuego is about 7,000 miles from my Florida home. How could I make such a long trip again?

"From Miami to Buenos Aires is—how many miles, Jorge?" I asked.

"By Pan American plane it's only 16 hours," he replied. "That's nothing."

"But from Buenos Aires here—" I started to protest.

Jorge grabbed a handful of little berries off a bush that grew along the stream, and popped a few into his mouth.

"Never mind the facts and figures," he said. "Try calafati."

"It's a wild berry," Bebe explained. "The Indians say that once you have tasted calafati, no matter how far away you may go, you'll always come back to Tierra del Fuego."

"Pass the calafati," I said, still counting miles in my mind. "All you've got."

I crammed a fistfull into my mouth. The berries began to stain our lips purple, but we chewed and chewed.

13. Fish-Filled Bahamas

Finny Finds around the islands provide plenty of light tackle sport. Tips on tackle, seasons, guides, and transportation.

WHEN I WENT to school they taught me to pronounce it Ba-HAW-mas, which is all very well, aside from the fact that the natives of this delightful territory call it "Ba-HAY-mas." The smaller islands, which in my book were Cays become, in the soft speech of the area, the "Keys." It's all rather confusing, but there's one point upon which no one ever argues. That's the fact that this little group of islands offers 70,000 square miles of fishing that is hotter than a Calypso singer going to town.

Around Nassau, down through the northern Bahamas, Andros Island, the Joulter Cays, the Berry Islands; over in the western Bahamas, at Bimini and Cat Cay, West End and Grand Bahama, and in the east, Eleuthera and the Exuma Cays there's so much fishing that in weeks—or even months—you can only scratch the surface.

Scattered all over the shallows are bonefish, permit (rare), crevalle jack and horse-eye jack, amberjack, yellowtail, blue runners, gaff topsail pompano, barracuda, mangrove and mutton snapper; even tarpon up to 40 pounds. Farther out are the rainbow-hued dolphin, the racy wahoo, albacore, tuna, oceanic bonito and mackerel.

If a fishing guy wants to feel the heft of a big billfish, there are the fierce-fighting white marlin—and gigantic, acrobatic

blue marlin. You'll find sailfish ready and willing. In the western Bahamas, from May to early June, the migrating bluefin
tuna move in around Bimini and Cat Cay; great powder-kegs
of fish, eager to sock the baits put to them by fast moving
charter boats.

As of a recent time, there were 33 standing world's record
fish taken in Bahaman waters; and there are still all sizes and
shapes of fish that would break those existing records, just
waiting to be caught. Down in the middle of Andros, Captain
Milton Pearce, who knows his fish and can judge their size,
says he has seen tailing and cruising bonefish that would go
between 18 and 20 pounds.

In the "blue holes"—deep spots like great lakes in the midst of
the flats—there are fish to make you cast and then duck. These
holes ranging from 100 feet to a half-mile in circumference,
are 10 to 40 feet deep. In them are ideal fish for light tackle;
tarpon, jack, snapper, grouper, big and little sharks, and all
kinds of things you don't expect.

Once while I was fishing a blue hole with Don McCarthy,
we got into some tarpon. They came out of there, streaking
for our surface lures, like bats out of a cave at dusk. One 35
pounder soared up, socked my popping bug and careened out
into the sunlight. Before he fell back he threw the bug a mile
into the air! Then Don had a hit and his reel began to scream
as that fish tore across the hole and slammed across the flat
for 250 feet on the far side before Don could stop him. We
knew it had to be a bonefish, and sure enough, it was—in the
middle of all those tarpon!

That's the way it is in the blue holes—fast fish and plenty
of action. Later I had a hit and fought it out for fifteen minutes
with a 5-pound jack. Just as I got that jack to the edge of the
hole, a 10-pound shark came from nowhere, grabbed him and
headed out. In a couple of seconds up bobbed part of the jack.
That shark had neatly cut it in half. Then, as I reeled that
top-half of the jack my way to free the hook, a 15-pound
cuda sliced up and finished the job. He nipped off everything

Guide William, at Walker's Cay, manufactures what was probably the first bonefish flag, when the author took a bonefish on a fly near that northern Bahama Island.

but a thin thread of gristle left hanging wistfully on the otherwise bare hook. I growled at both those hungry cusses but I knew that was the way of the sea dwellers, the big ones eat the little ones, and so on down the line.

My main interest when I first went to the Bahamas was bonefish and at the Bang Bang Club on Pot Cay in the north

bight of Andros Island, I found myself smack in the middle of
some of the best bonefishing to be found anywhere. There
are so many bonefish flats nearby that the guides never get
their parties far from the club. Within two miles of Bang Bang
we fished flats that no one had been on before: they'd been
too busy catching fish right on their doorstep.

At nearby Loggerhead Key and at Spanish Wells there are
tarpon that weigh around 40 pounds and that jump like sixty.
In the channels there are other finny finds that are as strong
as oxen and as bold as brass. Great horse-eye jacks follow your
lure to the boat and crevalle jack pull so hard you almost decide
to take to croquet.

I remember casting a surface popping bug there a couple of
feet from the shoreline. Before its tail feathers smoothed out,
a jack had it and was off on a dazzling run that made water
jump off the line. That jack ran like a jet for 250 feet, then
started shaking his head and boring away from me, broadside,
using his flat body to add to my discomfort. He was a tough
hombre, all right, but I outlasted him and got him in, a 6-pound
horse-eye jack with plenty of horsepower.

Another time, off Bang Bang with guide Joe Cokley, we
went out specially to tangle with barracuda. We found them
in two to four feet of water, lying like logs, a push-over for
a fast retrieve—but a double rodful, and no kidding!

I dropped a surface spinning lure well past, and eight or
nine feet in front of a basking cuda that looked as big as a
canoe. I started the lure back across the top, fast, making
water fly, so when it passed the cuda it was making plenty of
knots. That fish feigned sleep until the lure was ten feet past
him. Then he untied himself and launched his whole long body
through the air and on top of that fast-moving lure. When I
set the hook, all hell busted loose. I yelled and so did Joe and
the cuda started away in a series of jumps, five feet, then ten
—a sea-goin' cuda with the bit in his teeth. Right in the middle
of a jump the lure pulled loose and shot back our way like

a bullet. I ducked, retrieved it and reached for another. That fish had cut it neatly in half.

"He's still there!" shouted Joe.

"Tell him to wait," I shouted back, as I tied on the new popper.

I threw it five feet from that fish, never thinking he would hit it after the mix-up we had just had. But he wanted more excitement. From a standing start he leaped on that plug and started jumping right at the skiff. I kept striking and striking, hoping to get the hook home good and solid.

This fish seemed to go crazy! He jumped right at us and his second flight into the ozone carried him within a foot of us. He hit, threw water all over us and then dived under the skiff to cut the leader.

That pesky critter had a plug of mine and I wanted it back. Again I doubted that he would hit and now it seemed that he was gone for fair, but ten minutes later Joe Cokely spotted him. When I cast, this time using a wire leader, he hit again. I got him and retrieved my first plug. He weighed an even 14 pounds—a gimlet-eyed gangster with a mean attitude towards the world in general and fishermen's plugs in particular.

Out of Nassau I fished with Captain Milton Pearce. His boat is a 48-foot diesel job, which is perfect for trips to the outer islands. On one junket we cruised along Andros and stopped at Fresh Creek. After dinner we left the club and went a couple of hundred yards up the river and floated back with the tide. We were after tarpon, snapper, or jacks, and used spinning gear. On my third cast a tarpon rolled up and engulfed the top water lure. When I set the hook he busted out of there faster than an Atlantic salmon fleeing a seal. He was in and out, in and out, licking himself in a hurry, while I held on and hoped the 6-pound-test monofilament line would stand the racket. Suddenly he rushed the boat and jumped right over the stern, clearing it by less than a foot. I shuddered, and gripped the rod tighter but that play was the way out for this big

At Joulters Cay in the Bahamas, a hard fighting bonefish finally comes to net.

scaled buster. The line hit something sharp on the boat and bingo, he was gone.

I didn't have time to get a new lure on before I heard a shout from Don McCarthy and turned to see him fighting a fish that didn't show but that had just made a terrific boil beside the boat.

"What is it?" I asked him.

"Probably a big snapper," Don grunted. "I didn't see him."

"Look at that rod tip!" he said. The tip was shaking up and down.

"A jack!" he gasped. "And a big one!"

"All right," I said. "I'll take a nap for an hour. I know what those jacks are like."

"He's big all right," Captain Pearce agreed, as Don settled himself for a long tug of war.

It was fifteen minutes before he boated that 10-pound horse-eye jack.

Then we ran up the river and started our float again. We had four tarpon in the air in a hurry and wound up minus four lures as they frayed through the 10-pound test leaders. We just tied on new ones and tried again. Finally I managed to bring in a 10-pounder—but most of those 30 to 40-pounders we released about 70 feet behind the skiff! We didn't care. Who wouldn't have fun, just seeing them in the air?

We made a third run and drift, and as it was getting late we decided this would be our last. It was time to try for some sleep.

"Three more casts?" I asked.

"You bet," said Don.

"One!" we both cried, as we laid out long casts, and as if a pair of fish had been waiting there with open mouths, they had our lures. Once again we were off to the races.

That fish of mine was as stubborn as a mule. He pulled like one and he kicked like one and—like all mules—he upset the apple cart. I couldn't do a thing with him and he was always on the go. He ran and bored deep and ran some more. He didn't come near the surface. He made enough long runs to almost exhaust my line. I looked at the reel and gasped. Almost cleaned! I pulled back, dropped the tip, reeled fast. But pumping didn't work, either. Everytime I did that he just took more line. He finally took it all. Snapped it and went off with the works. The reel core was as bare as a bald head. I turned to Don. He stood there looking at me, shoulders shrugged, holding out his reel for my inspection. Cleaned, too!

"It's time for bed," I said.

"Yes," said Don. "It's too dark to put more line on now."

"It's midnight," said Captain Pearce. "And we are getting up at 4 a.m. to head for the Curly Cut Cays. Perhaps a bit of shuteye, gentlemen?"

He cranked the motor.

With a lot of this light tackle fishing there's the feeling that

Bonefish on, at Joulters Cay. Captain Milton Pearce guided the author into a tremendous school of fish that were waiting for high tide to put water on the flat. Note how the sand hills stand out in the shallows.

you are getting in on something new. When I first went to
Walker's Cay, I heard the guides singing a Calypso song that
went like this:

> *"Sweet little Walker Cay*
> *Sweet little Walker Cay*
> *You catch bonefish, marlin, tuna, dolphin,*
> *All in Walker Cay."*

Next morning I started out for bonefish with William Grant,
my Bahaman Negro guide. William was 18 and had five years
of guiding under his belt, but when I picked up my fly rod
at the dock, he shook his head.

"You can't catch bonefish on a fly," he said. "You gotta
use bait."

Having caught bonefish on flies in widely scattered parts of
the southern seas, I told him I'd like to try, anyway. He just
looked wise, and we shoved off and headed for the nearest
flat. We ran too close to the first one, and the bonefish, scared
by the motor, went out of there in waves. Then William cut
the motor, picked up the pole and we eased over to the next
flat, about 200 yards away. Immediately we saw a bonefish
tailing. I got ready to cast.

"They won't hit a fly. They won't hit a fly." William
chanted.

"We'll see," I chuckled, and dropped the fly three feet in
front of that busy grubber. He spotted it and rushed. I struck
and that haywire fish went loco for fair. He started off with
a couple of fast double 8's, did a straight-away dash for 50
feet, reversed and came back our way and passed the stern
of the skiff throwing mud and busting bubbles all about. That
fin-strong buzzard was racing along at a good 40 miles an
hour. He fairly flew! He kept on for 200 feet, slashed off
towards deeper water. Then I started slowing him down, getting line back. He coasted in, almost to the boat and got a

good look at William and me and twisted around and slipped across that flat as if he had seen 10,000 assorted birds of prey. He made his first effort look like a turtle crawl.

When I finally landed that five-pounder, I held it up for William's inspection.

"I believe you now," he said, all grins. "I believe you now. And how he took that fly, and how he run!"

That night as we got ready to go back to the Club, William lashed the poling pole to the side of the skiff, tied his handkerchief to the top, and we went in, sporting what was probably the world's first bonefish flag. Proudly William ran the skiff up beside the Sambo, natty fishing craft of George Bass, the famous big game angler, and all night long our improvised bonefish flag flapped in the breeze beside George's blue marlin flag.

The next day as I left Walker Cay I heard the Calypso singers sounding off with a new version of their song. It went:

"Sweet little Walker Cay,
Sweet little Walker Cay,
You catch bonefish ON A FLY, marlin, tuna, dolphin,
All in Walker Cay."

Some of the untold miles of fishing in the Bahamas are easily accessible; some call for lengthy trips by charter boat, and others are best reached by plane. Present-day travel in the Bahamas is fast and inexpensive, and it doesn't take long to find guides and arrange trips to the fishing grounds. Before you make plans, however, it's wise to study the seasons and areas where the fish you want are located. The following is a basic table from which you may work:

Central and eastern Bahamas: Andros, Joulter Cays, Berry Islands, Abaco, New Providence (Nassau), Eleuthera, Exuma Cays and Cat Island: amberjack—fall and winter; albacore, Allison tuna, oceanic bonito — summer; bonefish — all year around; blue marlin—spring and summer; wahoo—November through February; dolphin and kingfish—fall, winter and spring.

In the western Bahamas: Cat Cay, Bimini, West End, Grand Bahama and Walker Cay: amberjack—December through May; barracuda—all year round; bonefish—November through May for the larger fish and summer and fall for large schools of smaller fish; bluefin tuna—in the Cat Cay and Bimini areas, May 7 to June 10; blue marlin—stragglers from December through April and the best fishing in February, March and April; white marlin and sailfish—stragglers through the off season, plentiful during February, March and April; reef fish such as grouper, snapper, grunt and yellowtail—throughout the year with the cooler months offering best fishing.

For information on charter boats in the central and eastern Bahamas, get in touch with the Nassau Yacht Haven, Box 1216, Nassau, Bahamas, or Brown's Boat Basin, Box 716, Nassau. In the Western Bahamas: Chamber of Commerce Docks, 1310 Fifth Street, Miami Beach, Florida; Chamber of Commerce Docks, Fort Lauderdale, Florida; or West Palm Beach Fishing Club, West Palm Beach, Florida.

The Bahamas are within easy flying distance or steamer range of Miami. From that point, charter aircraft make Nassau in 50 minutes, while a steamer takes you there overnight. The New York to Nassau flight consumes 4½ hours, or, if you prefer to go by boat, there's direct sailing every Friday on the *S.S. Nassau*.

Regular flights go out of Palm Beach and Fort Lauderdale to Nassau and to Walker Cay, while charters from Miami will take you anywhere in the islands. For general fishing information, write to Don McCarthy, at the Development Board, Nassau, Bahamas.

14. Out Of This World

Fishing for snook in the awesome half-world of the Everglades Swamps of Florida.

THE BOW of the skiff rammed into an inch-thick vine that rode forward with us a bit, then thrust us back in our tracks. Capt. Boss Brown spun the outboard motor and gunned it hard, reversing at full speed toward a formidable array of clutching mangrove roots.

I dropped flat on my face, shoved my head under a seat, and clung to the bottom of the skiff. Back of me, amidships, George Phillips yelped, "This is worse than bucking a Kentucky line!" Then he ducked fast. Maybe Boss ducked too; I was too busy to look. But Boss is an awesome man and the mangroves probably parted and made way for him. Anyway he maneuvered out of that jumble and spun the motor forward again. Under me I felt the water swishing by smoothly, and thankfully raised my head for a gulp of air and a quick glance around.

The tunnel through which we were moving was so narrow that the water displaced by the boat pushed a wave high into the wall of mangrove trees on each side, and sucked an ebb tide behind us. It was like riding uphill on water. Even so, it was a channel, which was more than could be said for most of the route we had been following through the dusk-gloomy swamp for the past hour.

Boss Brown had looked grim when he met the four of us at the Rod and Gun Club at Everglades that morning in early February. Everglades is, of course, on the southwestern coast

169

of Florida, where the Gulf of Mexico seeps into the awesome half-world of the vast Everglades swamp.

"It's been blowing thirty miles an hour for three days," Boss said. "The water here is too muddy for anything but trolling, and I can see you guys don't want to troll."

He was eyeing our assorted fly and spinning rods. "Tell you what. Leldon and I can take you in two skiffs into the swamp —way back towards the headwaters of the rivers that empty into the Gulf here. It's tough going, but it's your only chance to get fish."

We started off in his forty-foot boat, towing two skiffs. Roaring between the islands through passages that were like great rivers among the mangroves, we slowed only occasionally to ease past a shallow oyster bar or to avoid shaking up a charter boat trolling the bays. For two hours, from just before daybreak till the sun was over the tallest mangroves, we ran through the pretzel channels and wide lakes where every surrounding vista was just as nature made it eons before.

We jumped birds by the hundred, including long-legged waders—the Ward's heron and the great white heron, once almost extinct here, but now making a strong comeback. Ahead of us, flocks of American egrets rose and flew until we passed, then settled back in the trees. The yellow-footed snowy ibis, the white ibis, and the clumsy wood ibis all rose in showers. Cormorants took off in front of us and coots ran across the surface, gathering speed to launch themselves into the air. Trash ducks, fish ducks, and edible ducks were everywhere.

Then, at the point of a bay, Boss tied the boat up against the mangroves and we took to the skiffs. That's how we came to be lying with our faces glued to the boards. Barely two yards wide and in most places only a few inches deep, the waterway cut through thick stands of red mangrove whose huge, crisscross roots wove a pattern so dense that an eel could hardly have squeezed between them.

Overhead the branches shut out the sky; we were truly out of this world. The air was thick with heat that bounced off the water, and thicker still with mosquitoes and sandflies. Occasionally a bird rose with a shattering flap of wings and tore along the channel ahead of us—the only course it could take through that maze of jungle.

Over everything hung the miasmic smell of the Everglades, an emanation of mulch and mist, of decaying fish and oysters and crabs and vegetation. It's like rotten eggs with a dash of vinegar thrown in. It smells terrible, but it grows on you till it's a good smell. It savors of the life, the struggle, and the strange, wild beauty of the Everglades.

Suddenly we flashed out of the tunnel into a prairie of sawgrass, spotted with clumps of palms and, in the distance, several of the famous Everglades "hammocks"—tree-clad islands sticking up amid the sawgrass. On the back of the skiff the motor jumped and squirmed and threw its hind end in the air as it struck a buried log, a hard mound of clay, or a submerged root. We looked back and saw Leldon's skiff laboring along behind us. Otto Shaw was crouched in the bow; all we could see of him were the fluttering streamers and skipping bugs clipped to his hat.

He unjointed himself enough to raise his head and take a squint forward and then we were again in a mangrove tunnel. Otto opened his mouth, took a big gulp of air, and went down again. But his partner, John Hunter, was not so quick. We heard a loud yell and turned to see John hanging in midair, snagged by tenacious vines, fore and aft. Boss threw our boat in reverse and we inched back.

By the time we got to him, John had extricated himself and was gasping for breath, both hands clutching his bruised throat.

"This" he croaked, "is kind of rough but I'll be O.K."

"The man they couldn't hang," said Otto, who got a dirty look from John.

We started forward again. Snook were somewhere not far ahead and all hell wasn't going to stop us. But it sure made a good try. We were no sooner under way than we heard another shout from behind. This time Leldon's motor had been mugged and yanked right off the skiff. As we watched, Leldon retrieved it from the mud and water and jammed it back into place. Then he tightened up its screws and pulled the starter cord. The motor spluttered but wouldn't catch.

"Hammer it," yelled Boss.

And before our popping eyes, Leldon did just that. Every time the panting, protesting motor faltered, Leldon hammered on the choke, forcing gasoline through where water was trying to take over, and driving the water out. On the fifth try the motor took hold.

Soon we reached another stretch of prairie grass and palms, where Leldon overtook us. On the far side huge cypresses rose a hundred feet in the air, and we knew we were near fresh water, where they thrive. We ran a short distance till we hit an acre of open water. We were just in time to see Leldon and his group disappear into a dark slit in the mangroves on the far side.

"There used to be some snook in here," said Boss, cutting the motor. "Big ones. Right around that little island. Snappers, too. Watch the water under those cormorants and you'll see something you never saw before."

Under the branches where the cormorants were perched, the leaves were white with guano. And even as we watched, droppings splashed into the water. As they hit, the snappers struck ferociously at them. Fascinated, we drew closer. Half-grown birds, black as a minstrel's face, edged uneasily in toward the tree trunks. One stumbled, fell into the water with a squawk, and frantically swam ashore.

"If they'll take guano, they'll take this," I said and tossed a fly beneath the branches.

It had barely hit the water before a foot-long snapper took it and came hurtling across the surface with the force of my strike. George picked up his spinning rod, threw a lure in and let it sink. Then he started to retrieve, but his line stopped solid.

"Bottom," he grumbled. "Can you put me in there, Boss, to free the line?"

Then suddenly the line came free of its own accord, while five pounds of snook busted out into the air and into the mangrove branches, then crashed back into the water, breaking the leader.

"Jumpy bottom," Boss grinned.

As we moved further along the island, George decided to try a surface spinning lure that is deadly on largemouth bass —one that he'd been anxious to try on snook. I stuck with my fly rod and skipping bug, casting toward the mangroves and bringing the rod down hard, almost to the surface, in order to shoot the bug a couple of feet under some overhanging branches. I let it sit there a bit, skidded it out and gave it a pop.

And then, from under the mangroves there shot a long, dark form; it went straight for the bug, took a wallop at it and missed, throwing water high. Somehow I managed to keep from striking. The next moment I couldn't have struck if I had wanted to. I stood there, arm aloft, like a statue, watching that snook make a frantic search for the bug. It tore the water into shreds and driblets, threw mud into the air as it scoured the bottom, midwater and surface—all at once, it seemed.

Then it came slowly out of the murky water and I saw the whole length of it. It lay there, thinking it over, pawing the mud with its anal fins, shaking and tossing its head, red-eyed as a mad bull. It looked formidable and somehow indestructible. It scared me.

But I wanted that fish on the end of my line. I gave the bug a slight pop and the monster charged, its dorsal fin and back cutting the surface, then went up in a long, looping leap, mouth open, teeth bared. It fell on that bug like a ton of bricks and I struck mightily—and missed! The bug flew high in the air. As I false-cast for another try I saw the snook again, ten feet away. But George saw it, too, and dropped his lure right in front of its long snout. The snook made a slow, majestic half-turn, like an ocean liner coming in to dock, opened its mouth to take—and saw us.

This time it dug a hole a foot deep in the muck and mire as it sprinted for the protective mantle of the mangrove roots.

Even Boss was awed.

"That's the biggest snook I've seen in many a long year. He must have weighed thirty-five pounds." He hesitated. "Yes, forty at least."

I sat down and was silent. What a chance I'd had—I'd probably never get another like it. As the years pass I may forget the fish I've landed, but I know I'll never forget that one I lost.

"Well," said Boss, "maybe we'd better get on where we're headed."

That was a lake in the New River country several miles below the famous Tamiami Trail, which cuts across the toe of Florida from the Atlantic to the Gulf. Lakes here are wide places in the maze of twisting guts, rivers and waterways. Some are small, others a mile or so long, but all are shallow. In them are snook, redfish, snappers, and the odd school of traveling jacks and tarpon. As the crow flies, we were only a little south of the Trail, and the water was mostly brackish. But the area is as remote as the craters of the moon to all but those who fight their way into it by boat, as we had, on a long, round-about course.

Leldon had got far ahead of us and when we chugged out into the remote lake we saw Doc Eaton standing on a seat in the skiff, fighting a fish—a big one, from the way his rod was bending.

"First cast!" he shouted at us. "He hit a popper on top. He's jumped twice already. Looks ten pounds."

Boss killed the motor and we sat back to watch Doc perform. He hung on, giving line when necessary, then laying back on his rod and handing that 6-pound test braided nylon spinning line everything he dared, alert for twists and turns and power dives. Once more the snook emerged into the Florida sunshine in a clean, arching jump, and slipped back in with scarcely a

In Key Largo Canal, a baby tarpon comes out in a spine-twisting leap.

splash. Then it came halfway out again and shook its head like a bulldog shaking a rag doll. It looked vicious.

Doc grinned. "Listen to him growl!" he said.

At last he eased the fish to the side of the boat, pulled its head out of water, and held it while Leldon produced a pair of pliers, clamped them onto the snook's lower jaw, and lifted it into the skiff. This was a new one on me. I'd seen most methods of landing fish and had improvised a few myself, but never anything like this.

"Snook are all over this rocky bottom," Leldon said. "It runs parallel to shore and about a hundred feet out. This is the second fish we've landed. Both about nine pounds."

"What are we waiting for!" shouted George.

Boss started the motor. So did Leldon, and both boats ran upwind to the middle of the lake. There the engines were shut off and we started casting. The boats drifted slowly along, about seventy feet apart. I had my favorite skipping bug on and my first cast got a strike from a three-pounder that tore up and engulfed the bug, acting as if it wanted to swallow leader and fly rod and maybe me, too. It jumped twice, but on the security of a ten-pound-test tippet I roughed it in, took the hook out, and put it back. I had another cast in the air before it could find its pals to tell them the bad news. But it must have used mental telepathy because I didn't get another strike for a quite awhile, and neither did George.

Finally George changed lures, putting on an underwater spinner. This particular yellow-bodied, yellow-tailed number, had hardly started back George's way when something thumped it hard. A snook long enough to know better came roaring out of the water, shaking that lure like fury, and then threw it right back at George, a fast ball with a hop on it. Before the echo of the splash had faded, I had a fly in the air while George reeled fast, trying to get line back on his spinning reel so he, too, could try for that baby again.

Then we heard the screech of a reel from the other boat and saw John's flyrod bent almost double as his fish sounded and tore along the bottom in a long, sustained run. It was a big fish, with extra sharp gill covers that it used expertly to cut through the ten-pound test nylon leader and make off with the streamer John was using.

Most of us were talking as hard as we were fishing, but Doc Eaton, supposedly the novice of the trip, just quietly kept his lure in the water, with hardly ever a word. Pretty soon we discovered that he had three snook, each weighing over 9 pounds, while tops for the rest of us was not even 4 pounds. We began talking about the big ones we'd caught on some other trip, in some other water. The harder a fish fought, the more we recalled a stronger fish elsewhere. Poor Doc just sat there fishing and occasionally looking at his 9-pounders, plugging along, humming a tune to himself, and having fun.

Time went by and we were beginning to relax after our strenuous trip to the lake. My bones were sore here and there and John's neck showed a swollen red welt, but considering what we'd been through, we felt all right. Then, when strikes fell off, Leldon shouted, "Let's go!"

"Not another ride through the tunnel of love!" groaned Otto.

Leldon cranked up, and roared away wide open, headed for another lake.

"This time," said Boss, "we'll let him lead. It's the worst passage yet."

"Oh no!" I said. "How about staying here? We're having a good time."

"There's a big one, where Leldon's going. About 30 pounds," Boss answered. "We just have time to try for him."

Who could turn down a pass at a 30-pound snook? We took off after Leldon, congratulating ourselves that the other boat would now take the brunt of any spider webs, logs, and alligators that might be cluttering up the passage. George and I took our favorite positions, flat on the bottom, and it was just as well we did. Big, sloppy mangrove branches swished across the top of the skiff, ready to level everything they hit, whether it was a head or an arm or the end of a fly rod. Somehow one branch got under the midship seat and prodded me smartly in the stomach before it tore loose. I saw George squash a couple of inch-wide spiders that dropped off it.

"While you're at it," I suggested, "toss overboard that little green snake there by your elbow."

George looked down, snatched, and threw, and the next second I thought he must have been bitten.

"Yowie!" he yelled. "Give 'er the gun. Let's get out of here."

I raised my head just enough to look where his popping eyes were staring over the edge of the boat. As we skimmed by, I looked full into the baleful gaze of a six-foot cottonmouth. The little green snake, half stunned, was lying right in front of it. Apparently George had thrown it right in the moccasin's face!

Behind me I heard Boss chuckling: "Bet you never looked a cottonmouth right in the eye before."

George and I grunted and rearranged ourselves under the seats.

"We're almost there," announced Boss, at last.

"Why, it's only been years," said George. "I thought this went on forever."

History repeats itself, they say, and sure enough, when we came into this lake where the big snook was supposed to live, there was Doc standing on the seat and fighting another fish. His rod was bent and he was intent on what was going on underwater. Boss killed the motor and paddled toward the other boat.

"Biggest one yet," yelled Otto. "About fifteen pounds."

"Bring him in, Doc," John was shouting. "How can I ever get to fish when you've always got one on? Quit fooling with him. Give him the butt."

Then that fish decided to go for the mangroves, 200 feet away. He made it in one run, while Doc fought back with all the drag he dared. Leldon pulled over to the mangroves, while Doc worked at keeping a tight line.

"He's deep in the roots!" he cried.

"Hold him," Leldon urged. "Maybe we can work him out."

"He'll never get that snook," George told me. "It's sure to cut the line on something."

We both got up and started casting. I had a hit and landed a 2-pounder. George brought in one that looked to be about 7 pounds. For ten minutes we paid no attention to the others. Then we heard shouts from the shore. All three of them—Doc, Otto and John—were standing in the skiff and Leldon was out on the mangrove roots.

"Let's go in," I said to Boss. "I believe that fish is still on. Maybe Doc can land him yet."

We pulled up alongside the other boat.

"He's only about ten feet in now," Otto said. "Doc's getting him out. Leldon went across the roots and turned him this way."

We watched, fascinated, as inch by inch that fish came out. Doc kept on such steady pressure that we wondered how much seesawing across mangrove roots his line could take. But at last the fish swam out from the iron-fingered roots and into the lake. Leldon leaped back into the skiff and paddled toward deeper water, with Doc keeping the pressure on. The fish was almost ready now.

Then Leldon reached into his hip pocket and came out with the pliers. We all groaned.

"Hit him on the head with them!" I shouted.

"And knock him off the hook?" Leldon snorted.

He grabbed the leader in one hand and held the fish still, got a grip with the pliers on the lower jaw, and lifted it into the skiff.

"About 14 or 15 pounds," Boss drawled.

"Let's go!" suddenly Leldon shouted. "We can just get out before dark."

He gunned the motor and shot down the lake, heading for a small hole in the wall of mangroves. I edged under the seat, closed my eyes and held my hands over my ears.

15. Angler's Choice

Whatever we named those Florida guides could produce!

ABOUT A MILE from shore, out on the shallow reefs, Angus Boatwright stopped the cruiser. He baited up a couple of small spinning reels with small pieces of cut bait.

"We'll start small," he told us. "Catch your own bait. We want about 20 grunts, for big fish bait."

We cast out the bits of cut bait and waited. Not long. Before the bait had fairly settled we were into a couple of hard thumping little "grunts," favorite bait of most charter boats that are out for big stuff on the Florida Keys. They were good sport, too, on the little light fresh water outfits with Johnson Century reels that Angus had provided. In short order we had the 20 grunts that Angus had stipulated.

He started the motor.

"First," he said, "we'll get 40 to 60 pound amberjack. We'll find a school, get them on top and hold them there."

I looked at Angus. It seemed to me he was calling his shots pretty close.

Just then he turned the fathometer on. It was a flashing type, with a circle of red dots that flashed signals showing the depth beneath us. As we watched, we saw an oblong black spot move across the screen.

"Whew!" snorted Angus. "Did you see that?"

"You mean that was a fish?" I whispered, as if that thing down there might hear me.

"And what a fish!" said Angus.

He threw the motor out of gear, filched a grunt from the live well, impaled it on a hook and handed me the rod.

"Are you in good condition?" he asked.

"Wonderful, . . ." I stated. Then, thinking of that oblong shadow we had seen, I pulled in my horns a little. "Fair," I said.

I dropped the grunt over and watched the line free spool out until it hit the bottom. Then I threw the reel in gear and reeled line in until I knew the grunt was swimming free. Right then the line went down, with a bang.

"Strike!" yelled Angus.

I struck, and felt like I'd been hit with a hammer. There was a good drag on the reel and for a few minutes it was a tug of war to see whether I'd get that baby headed up or he'd get me headed down. But tackle told, and eventually up he came.

"Here," shouted Angus. "Take this. Give me your outfit."

Into my hands he shoved another rod with a live grunt dangling from the leader.

"I can keep the whole school up here by holding this fish out there. If I bring him in, they'll all leave."

I dropped the fresh grunt overboard. It had hardly hit before there was a flash of silver and another amberjack was heading for the bottom. I fought this one long and hard before I finally got him near the boat.

"Hold it," said Angus. "Let me land this one, and then I'll get another line ready for you."

"Listen, Angus," I said. "I believe you about the amberjack. You called it. And it looks to me as if this could go on all day. Let's land these two, and then go see what else you have to offer."

I brought the big amberjack to the side of the boat. Still holding my first fish out there in the water, Angus leaned over, grabbed this one by the gill and pulled him up.

A hundred pound tarpon strikes to the big streamer cast by the author, as Captain Leo Johnson handles the skiff. Ten jumps later the big silver king threw the hook.

"Fifty-seven pounds," he said, putting it on the scale. "Now let's see what the other one goes."

"Forty-two pounds," he said, when he had it in.

Standing there at the side of the boat, holding 99 pounds of fish in his hands, he looked at me.

"Want to turn them loose?" he asked.

I nodded.

He dropped them so they went into the water head first and we saw them swim away.

"That way, they'll go right down," said Angus. "But if I had dropped them in tail first, they would be full of air and wouldn't sink. Sharks would get them."

"Let's try for 50 pound black groupers now," he said, straightening up.

I nodded. After what I had just seen, I figured that if Angus said we were going to get 50 pound black groupers, Angus knew what he was talking about.

The propeller spun and we steamed away. Not far out we passed Captain Bill Smith's charter boat, the *Bilbon*. My friend Jean Crooks was standing on the bow, his rod pointed straight down.

"Big amberjack," he yelled. "He's giving me a fit. Had him for 30 minutes now."

"Spinning outfit," Bill added, pointing at Jean's rod. "Live grunt on spinning outfit. He'll be busy for quite a while."

I grinned as we steamed away. Remembering the punch those amberjacks had packed, even on a big outfit, I was mighty sure that, like Bill said, Jean would be busy for quite a while.

We stopped.

"Grouper grounds," said Angus.

We caught black groupers from 45 to 50 pounds. After three of them, I was ready for anything—anything else, that is. My arms were spent rubber bands and my legs were rubberier than that.

"Jewfish," said Angus, the next time he stopped the boat. "Hundred pounders."

This time he handed me an outfit so heavy I could hardly heft it. I pulled at the drag he had set on that reel and couldn't budge it.

"What kind of a drag is this?" I wanted to know.

"It's nothing," said Angus. "Nothing at all."

He baited up, took the rod and free spooled line out, then handed the outfit back to me. Finally the line stopped and I reeled in a few yards.

"How will I know when I have a hit?" I asked.

"It will feel just like I jumped on the end of the rod," said Angus.

And just then it happened.

Angus' description hadn't been too good. It was more as if I were tied to a slow moving freight train. Before I knew it, I was being pulled out of the fighting chair, slowly but surely. I braced my feet against the stern and hung on, but forward I went, across the deck to the stern, right up on top of the transom, almost overboard. Out of the corner of my eye, all the while, I could see Angus doubled over, laughing. Finally I got the drag lessened and adjusted and then I was able to get back in the fighting chair and relax a bit. But even with the lighter drag I was pulled out of the chair again and again. I hadn't thought that anything could put a bend in that telegraph pole I was using for a rod, but this fish did it.

Finally I got him coming up. I pumped some more and after weathering several dives at last brought this monster of the deep topside. Angus put the gaff to him and I laid the rod down and helped pull that big jewfish into the boat. He weighed 125 pounds.

"You and your 'nothing at all' drag!" I said. "That fish all but took me overboard."

Just then we heard Bill Smith's voice on the ship to shore radio.

"Jean's got his fish," he said. "Forty-two pounds. On spinning tackle and a 12 pound test line. That's a nice catch."

"A wonderful catch," Angus and I agreed.

A wonderful catch, typical of the wonderful fishing along these Florida Keys, that fantastic string of islands running from Miami to Key West. Where else could we go and listen to a man call every fish we caught and even name the weight within a couple of pounds.

"Wish we had time to go out to the Gulf Stream and look for a patch of seaweed," Angus was saying. "You can have a lot of fun casting to the dolphin that lie under the weeds. And they're like the amberjack. Get one on and keep him near the boat and you can hold the whole school."

The next morning we went out from Whale Harbor with Captain Howard Victor aboard his boat *The Cadet*. Destination?—you bet—the edge of the Gulf Stream, where the floating weed patches were. Object?—you bet—dolphin.

As soon as we reached the Sargasso weeds, floating there in a long string with thicker patches here and there, we had action.

A 7-pounder hit and jumped. We reeled it to within 30 feet of the boat and kept it there so that the school would follow. I reached for a fly rod, and made a cast into the vivid, swimming splashes of color where the school of following fish darted here and there around their hooked fellow.

I took three, all around 8-pounds before they left. On the next school we used spinning outfits and had the same luck. Then we went quite a way without a hit. Then a fish hit in a smother of flying water, and jumped. This was no school fish, it was at least 20 pounds. I fought him on the 4 ounce tip and the 20 pound test monofilament line. It took 30 minutes on the dot to land him.

A bit later a 25 pounder hit. He took 40 minutes to land.

We took several more before it was time to head in. Once again these Keys captains had called it right.

It is this amazing consistency that makes Florida Keys fishing what it is. There are certain fish there, year round, and they are "habit fish"—you can find them in certain localities almost every time. And besides these permanent residents there are the tourists that come in seasonal waves, migrating, spawning, or just passing through. The Islamorada Fishing Guides' Association has the comings and going of their fish so well charted that if anglers follow the time schedule they can be almost certain of getting in on the fishing they want. They're as regular as a Pan American Airlines schedule.

A fairly complete roster of fish that are found year round in Key's waters would include amberjack, mackerel, grouper, snapper, barracuda, muttonfish, albacore, bonito, dolphin, jack, permit, ladyfish, yellowfin tuna, African pompano, cobia, spotted sea trout, snook, mako, some sailfish, redfish, bonefish and dock tarpon. The added high spots provided by seasonal swimmers start in November when the sailfish move into the Keys area from more northern waters. They are followed by kingfish and wahoo, and all hit their high season throughout December, January, and into February and March. In April all the shallow water fish start to work better. The bonefish move in on the flats in ever increasing numbers and there are more redfish or channel bass on the Gulf side of the Keys and there is an inshore migration of muttonfish. About the same time, the fabulous migration of big tarpon, from 50 to 200 pounds, starts, running through May. In June the white marlin start working the Gulf Stream, big dolphin show in increasing numbers, and there are lots of albacore and bonito. Towards the end of the month the big tarpon begin to thin out.

In July and August there are sails, bonito, albacore and some blue marlin working hard on the great schools of bait in the Stream, small fish that look like menhaden, and on schools of houndfish. This activity dwindles into September, when the calendar lists great bottom fishing, and inshore angling for bonefish, ladyfish and some snook. By November the cycle is complete and sails are moving down from the north again and dolphin work the currents or seas and bigger bonefish move in. By December, sailfishing is again at its peak.

Of course, weather can beat anyone. Excessive wind and cold will usually hurt the fishing. Yet so consistent are the movements of fish and so thoroughly have they been studied by the Keys guides that not only can they pick the place and size of the bottom dwellers, as Angus did for me that day, they can often even select the size of such flashy swimmers as the sailfish.

Last November Lyman Rogers and I went out with Captain Eddie Edenfield on his *Lady Luck II.*

"I've caught sails before," said Lyman. "But what I want today is a trophy fish. One that's small enough to hang above our mantel."

"About 10 pounds?" asked Eddie.

"That would be nice," grinned Lyman. "Think you can arrange it?"

"There've been plenty of small ones around," said Eddie. "We'll do our best, anyway."

We started trolling. We had three lines out, one from each out-rigger, and a flat line, straight back for 40 feet. We were hardly settled in our chairs before there was a shout from Eddie.

"Sail! Back of your bait, Lyman. A small one."

Lyman tensed, watching the action.

The sail moved in, tapped the bait, and Lyman yanked the line from the outrigger and when it came tight, he struck. Nothing was there. He reeled fast, trying to make that fish think its prey was escaping. It worked. The sail showed again, and hit. Lyman free spooled and dropped the bait back and gave the fish a chance to swallow it.

"Give it time," said Eddie.

Then we saw the line moving forward and when it came tight between rod and fish, Lyman struck.

It was a little beauty of a sail that came busting out on top and did a rumba that made his dorsal swing from side to side. He tailwalked, then went under but came right up again. He jumped a dozen times, cut the water every which way. But after a last wild flurry, he faded fast and Lyman got him boatside. Eddie grabbed the leader wire, got a grip on the spike of a bill and hoisted that game little buster aboard.

"About 8 pounds," said Eddie. "You got your mount."

"Even those little ones can really turn it on," said Lyman, after he was baited up again and back in his fighting chair. "Eddie, how did you know there would be a small one around today? How did you know I wouldn't get a big one?"

"Maybe you will!" yelled Eddie. "Watch your bait!"

We all saw it. Eight feet of sailfish snatched that bait like it was gold, turned and went into high. He looked as if he would never stop. He went a hundred yards in 10 seconds flat. Then he took to the air, leaping away from us, four, five, six times, tearing gaping holes in the face of the ocean with deep-forked tail. Then he stood on his caudal and danced away, tail-walking for twenty feet and knocking the top of the waves into spindrift. This spindle-snouted deep sea racer was wide open.

Lyman was clamped down on him, braced in the fighting

Mrs. Hank Andrews, wife of the Outdoor Writer for the Cleveland Press, brings a sail in.

chair, ready for anything. The 20 pound test monofilament was slicing the water, an invisible strand, but doing some pulling of its own.

And then, far out, that great sailfish struggled skyward again, and we all saw what happened.

"That's it!" shouted Lyman. "He's thrown the hook."

He reeled in his empty line. Eddie and I kept looking sternwards. That had been a bigger than average sail, a giant among his brethren. As if to really show us, he came out again, free this time, in a beautiful high jump, a sort of goodbye wave to us. Automatically the three of us raised our right hands in a silent salute, a reverent tribute to a fish as game as they come. Lyman walked over to his little 8 pounder and patted it.

"Your pappy got away," he said.

Of course, not everyone catches his fish by appointment, as we did on the two trips just described. A lady named Evelyn Griffith, of Boston, was fishing blind alongside one of the Keys bridges last winter, using dead shrimp. Suddenly something snatched up the bait, zipped southward parallel to the shore, cutting through the water at a startling pace. Evelyn held on, hardly able to believe that anything that swims could go so fast. Then the speeding fish dashed back her way.

"It went by me like a jaguar," she said later. "The line was smoking. The water around it seemed on fire."

Then, as she hung on, the reel handle flew off and disappeared into space.

"I grabbed the line with my bare hands and started hauling," she said. "And then that fish showed. It was nothing I had ever seen before, and I was determined to get it in. I kept hauling and after a while I got him in shallow water and ran out knee deep and grabbed him. But he slipped through my fingers, so I got a firm grip on the line and started running for shore."

The fish couldn't take that and this time the lady dragged him far up on the sand. Anxious to find out what her quarry was, she picked the fish up in her arms and started down the road. She spotted three linemen working on a telegraph pole.

"What is this fish?" she called up to them. "I just caught it."

"That's a bonefish," one of them replied. "One of the best game fish in the ocean. And a big one, too."

"He weighed 9½ pounds," said Evelyn proudly. "Away above average."

So game is the bonefish that many Florida Keys guides hate to see them killed, and most are returned to the water. Stalking bonefish on the shallow flats and casting to him is like shooting at a particularly difficult target, because he is always on the move. In fact, one way the guides will instruct you to distinguish between a bonefish and a barracuda or other shallow water swimmer, is to tell you that if the fish you see is not on the move, it is not a bonefish.

Most guides fish for bonefish with live shrimp for bait, the guide casting the bait to such a position that the approaching fish picks up the scent and goes to the shrimp. Light tackle is used and the combination provides as sporty a type of skiff fishing as can be found anywhere. A growing contingent also go for Mr. Bonefish with artificial spinning and fly lures, and in this case the thrill of the hunt and the fabulous fight is intensified. Veteran fisherman and guide alike are carried away. I remember one bonefish that was feeding in ten inches of water when we spotted him, his tail protruding above the surface as he nosed into the bottom for some tasty morsel. With the sun at my back I could see the whole outline of his body, and at his head the puff of mud he put up as he snorted into the soft bottom.

"Get ready," whispered guide Lee Vondersar as he poled the skiff carefully towards the busy fish.

At 65 feet I false cast line out and shot the fly on its way. The small white bucktail lit two feet in front of the fish and he spotted it fast. There never was any doubt about that baby's intentions. He rushed the fly and before I had made two strips of the line he fell all over it and threw water high as he took and turned. When I struck, he went wild.

He charged right at us, saw the boat, turned on a dime and zipped right back where he had been. But he didn't like it there either, and to show his disapproval he went into a figure 8, unwound, did another, then read the chart right and this time headed for the deepest part of the ocean. He slammed through those shallows like mad, throwing up sand and busting bubbles in his wake, like the tail stream of a jet. The line was coming off the reel like it was evaporating into thin air and I couldn't see the reel handle, the spool was spinning so fast.

"Careful!" said Lee. "Let him run!"

"Let him run!" I thought. How could I stop him?

And I didn't even want to stop him. This was the top thrill in angling, a speeding bonefish on his way, and the feel of him and a beautiful working fly rod and reel.

"Yippee!" I yelled.

And in back of me I heard Lee. "Yippee! Yeow!"

Captain Al Lipford of Islamorada, Florida, "bills" a sail.

We were veteran bonefishermen, but like always, bonefish set us on fire.

That crazy bonefish went 600 feet before he stopped his rollicking run. It was another 20 minutes before I finally brought him in, and then he was still fighting. When we put him back in the water, Lee had to hold him upright, and give him artificial respiration, making side to side swipes, to pull water through the gills of this wonderful fish, so game he almost killed himself with his all out fight.

The bonefish is the most spectacular and hard fighting of any of the shallow water fish along the Florida Keys, but in the "back country," roughly meaning the Florida Bay country from the main Keys back west to Sandy Key and north and west to the Florida mainland—this back country is a fantastic fish pond for light tackle anglers.

It is a region of shallow flats, small channels, small lakes or "holes" in the flats, running from four to 12 feet deep, ideal hideouts for redfish, ladyfish, snook, mangrove snappers, spotted sea trout and barracuda. The fish are there year round, with the top fishing time being in the spring when concentrations of spawning fish seem to be everywhere. But almost any time you can come up with a bagful of eating fish as well as some of the fighters such as the ladyfish, whose main claim to interest is the flashy show they put on when hooked.

Like deep water guides, those who take you into the back country can pretty well spot the species and size of fish you are likely to get. Last time Dick Williams took me over to Johnson Key he promised me ladyfish, redfish and snook.

"We'll start with ladyfish and redfish, likely," he said.

"Afraid to stick your neck out?" I asked. "What do you mean, 'likely'."

He laughed.

"Well, I don't like to be too definite. Once in a while we do get skunked. What I really meant was that the redfish are out on the flats and the ladyfish are in the channels and we

have to work through them before we hit the spots where
the snook lie, along the shores of the Keys."

The ladyfish and redfish were there, providing the first line
of defense, all right. I was using a fly rod popper and Dick told
me to drop it over in a channel about 60 feet away. The second
it hit there was a streak of silver under it. I struck and out
came a long, lean ladyfish, a 3-pounder, big for the species, a
bundle of animated dynamite, playing hopscotch all over the
surface. No fish can go in and out of the water as fast as a
ladyfish, zigging and zagging and switching ends until the rod
is tied in knots. We had ten minutes of that kind of forked
lightning display before Dick finally netted the lady.

"Look what's coming," he said, as he released the fish.

Ninety feet away, on the other side of the channel, in two
feet of water, a school of fish was moving towards us, pushing
a wave in front.

"Redfish!" I yelled.

I bit the popper off, grabbed a streamer fly and tied it on,
and still had time to drop the fly a couple of feet ahead of
the oncoming school.

"That's right," said Dick. "Put it right on their noses or
they'll never see it. They're so short sighted they need bifocals."

But one of that school must have had his bifocals on, because
he spotted that fly and grabbed it. I felt his hit and I struck so
hard that he felt mine, too. The whole school flushed with him.

That red devil ran 200 feet, then put his nose down in the
muddy bottom and started to rub it back and forth, trying to
dislodge the fly, a characteristic tactic of the redfish. He must
have dug a hole a foot deep before he gave up and took out
again. This time he stopped after 50 feet and then started
shaking his head back and forth, as if saying, "No! No!"

I gave him line and he fell out of that act, and at last I got
tightened up again and got him coming. Now I really put it
to him, hauling, pumping, and finally giving the rod hard, short
jerks that addled his brain. It worked.

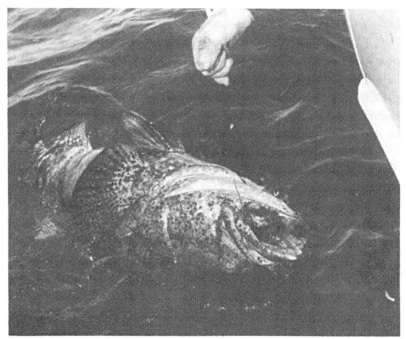

The 125 pound jewfish that almost pulled the author overboard, finally comes to boat.

I reeled him in, Dick put the net under him and slowly lifted him from the water.

"Twelve pounds," he said. "A real good redfish."

He slid old red back into the water.

"Now we'll go for that snook," he said.

We moved in to within casting distance of the shoreline. I used the same fly as I had for the redfish, a big red and yellow streamer tied on a 1/0 hook, with four-inch long wings that worked on the retrieve.

I cast to the stumps along the shoreline for ten minutes without a strike. Then a 2-pound mangrove snapper got in the act and socked the fly hard. I got him in, and we kept that one to eat.

The next stump produced a hit, too, but I didn't connect. The fly came right back at me and made me duck. In where the fish had swirled was a boil of water as big as a punt.

"That's a snook," said Dick. "Rest him a minute."

He poled out a few yards and staked out. I changed to a streamer with long white wings, red hackles, and a white chenille body.

"Change of menu," I said. "Maybe he'd remember the other one."

We waited ten minutes, then eased back in.

The fly hit just right and I didn't even have time for a strip. That snook hit so hard that the force of his attack carried him half way out of the water. We had a good view of his upper half.

"Golly!" said Dick in a whisper.

I couldn't talk. That snook was 15 pounds at least.

He tore down the shoreline, just missing a couple of stumps, and then he came out.

"Twenty pounds!" yelled Dick.

Then that baby turned for the deep and shot out into the channel. He went down, neared the far side and zoomed up again. He hit the flat and tore across it. Finally he slowed and I put the butt to him. He kept pointing away from me, making big swipes with his tail, gaining a foot each time. Then he was off. He had frayed through the leader with that sharp edge he carries on his gill covers.

"Too bad," said Dick. "He was a nice one. But let's try for the sea trout now."

But we never did get to the sea trout. A school of 100 pound tarpon came by and we were busy with them till time to head back across the bay to the Keys. We had them in the air. We had them here and there and everywhere but in the boat. And a couple of times, we nearly had them in the boat, too.

There's nothing in the world, even in these fabulous Keys, quite like the spring migration of big tarpon into the shallow waters of the Bay of Florida.

Some small silver kings, called yard or dock tarpon are found year round in channels, around bridges, in canals. But in April the hordes of heavyweight spawners move in. They hang around throughout most of June before continuing a westward

Mrs. Hank Andrews of Cleveland, and Captain Howard Victor admire a 55 pound sailfish caught by Mrs. Andrews.

trek, and while they are on the Keys there is a sudden frantic activity as fishermen pour in, day and night, to sample this marvellous fishing. They go for them with live bait, dead bait, trolling, still fishing and by all the casting methods. Many giants are taken by trolling, and some from the bridges, but back in the bay on the Gulf side, the wild-eyed brigades of light tackle men go after them with plug, fly and spinning gear, and make some sensational catches.

You wouldn't think a guy could lay it on the line for those big tarpon, but Jerry Coughlan, a real gone angler from Essex Falls, N.J., and Jimmie Albright, his guide, can more or less call their shots. Jerry uses a small plug casting rod, 18 pound test line, and a regulation plug casting reel, and he fishes only for tarpon over a hundred pounds. For eight years running he has copped the bunting for the biggest tarpon in the plug casting division of the famous Metropolitan Miami Fishing Tournament. He has landed 35 silver clad thunderbolts over a hundred pounds, his top fish on that wispy 18 pound test line going 161 pounds 8 ounces. This year's winner was 135 pounds, Jerry's own weight when soaking wet.

And by the time Jerry hangs a tarpon over 100 pounds, he is soaking wet, for sure.

One day I watched him fight three such busters, starting with the first fish we saw that morning. Jerry dropped his top water plug six feet in front of that oncoming tarpon and gave it action. The tarpon zoomed up, opened his big mouth and inhaled. As the fish turned, Jerry struck. Then that tarpon went wild. He made a tremendous swirl, got a finhold in the water and flung himself up and out, up for four feet, his gill rakers rattling, his long, thick body writhing, as if trying to lift himself upwards still further by his fins. Right in front of us, 40 feet out, he looked as big as a barn door. When he fell back in, it sounded like a great wave crashing on a beach.

For a moment he seemed stunned but he got his wind and shot off away from us. After 100 feet he went into a series of greyhounding jumps, a wild, silver torpedo going places. Then we saw the plug sail high in the air.

An hour later Jerry landed and released a 90 pounder. Another hour and he boated one that went 128 pounds, a fine fish that won the tournament that year.

We went in then. All around us other skiffs and charter boats were heading in, too. The sun was melting on the horizon, the way it does down there in the Gulf. Another day for silver kings was drawing to a close. And it was the last fishing day of the season for Jerry. He was heading north the next morning.

I noticed his lips moving.

"Counting the number of tarpon you landed this year?" I asked.

"Counting the days," he grinned. "Counting the days until the tarpon move into the Keys again next April."

16. *Mexican Dividend*

Unexpected returns to an angler who was just filling in time while waiting for a boat.

IT TOOK only a few minutes to go through the customs at Nogales and after we crossed into Mexico the roads were wide open with nothing to slow us down but an occasional burro and the odd vacquero crossing the macadam. We by-passed Hermosillo, the only large town en route, and by four o'clock we were in Guaymas.

We drove right to the docks at the Miramar where I had been told that Tom Jamison had a fleet of charter boats to cater to the guests at the lodge there as well as the Hotel Playa de Cortes, next door, where we were to stay while we fished the teeming waters of the Gulf of Lower California for the big yellowtails that I'd heard were out there.

But Tom had bad news.

"Why didn't you let me know you were coming?" he said. "Most of the time we have several boats free, but right now everything's tied up for two days. The place is loaded with fishermen from California, here for the weekend."

"But you might try some shore fishing," he said. He waved an arm towards Bacochibampo Bay, right in front of us. "Try some casting from those stone jetties over there to the left. You might get corbina and may be some sierras—Spanish mackerel. I'll get you a boat as soon as I can, but I'm afraid you're going to have to wait until Monday."

201

The author took this 12 pound corbina within 100 yards of the Playa
de Cortes Hotel, casting from the jetties and using an American type
spinning reel, the Johnson Century, and a goldfish lure.

I went over to the Hotel Playa de Cortes, got settled,
grabbed a spinning rod, a box of lures, and headed for the jetties. Tom hadn't been too promising but at least I wouldn't
entirely waste the two days if I could get a few fish along the
shore.

There were four rock jetties running out a hundred feet
into Bacochibampo Bay. I eased out over the sharp rocks of
the end jetty and threw out a white bucktail jig.

I had just started to retrieve when I saw a dark shape right
in back of my lure. I worked the lure hard, made it jump and
jerk, but the shape just stayed with it, didn't hit. Then right
in front of me, the shape took form. It came to the surface,
shook himself, and swam away. It was a waterbird—a least
grebe.

On my next cast I had a hit at once and it was no bird, this
time. I pulled in a two pound sierra. That little mackerel fought
hard enough to cheer me up a bit. Maybe I was going to get
some good fishing this weekend, boat or no boat.

I threw out again and caught a three pound corbina, a member of the croaker family. Then I cast for ten minutes without a strike.

I decided to try a bigger lure, and began casting a half ounce gold spoon towards the end of the jetty on my right. I figured the water was about ten feet deep there, so I let it sink a good way, then started it back in a slow, even retrieve. Suddenly it stopped dead, the rod tip went slowly and evenly down.

"A rock," I thought. "I'm fouled up."

Then the rod tip began to bounce. This was no rock. The fish was headed for the middle of the bay. He took fifty feet of line before he slowed enough to allow me to put on the brakes and turn him. He turned then, all right, but as soon as he was facing me, he started shaking his head and switching his body back and forth. I had to ease up on him for fear he'd break me up if I held him too hard. He went deep, then, and ran slowly to the left. After a bit, I turned him again and this time he swam my way and I had to crank the Johnson Century reel feverishly, trying to keep a tight line. In close, he shook some more and again I had to give line. But I tightened before he could turn away and he was tired now and I reeled him in closer. He came to the top and I saw the length of him, a big silvery corvina. A good one!

I had no gaff or net so I reeled him in to four feet from the rod tip and then clambered along the rock jetty towards shore, leading the fish. At the end of the jetty I jumped down to the sandy beach and skidded him up on it.

"A beauty!" said a voice in back of me. "Let me weigh him for you."

A fisherman who apparently had just come down over the cliff behind me, grabbed the corbina and put him on the scale he had in one hand.

"Twelve pounds one ounce," he read. "That's a nice fish. That's one of the best I've seen taken off the jetties."

It was nearly dark then, so I walked back to the Playa, thinking over the situation as I went. Perhaps I was going to enjoy

Hank, who operates Hank's Boat Livery at Guaymas, took the author
to a hot spot in the middle of town, and brought out a few pargo like this
beauty.

some extra fishing here that I hadn't expected. Maybe this was not going to be a lost weekend after all.

I buttonholed Jose Mauriquez, the charter boat dispatcher at the hotel.

"Tell me a little about the shallow water fishing here, from shore," I said. "Is there any other place as good as those jetties?"

"Hank," he said. "Go and see Hank."

Hank operated a skiff rental service over at the end of the beach. He looked interested when I said I wanted to fill in a couple of days with light tackle onshore fishing.

"I know a few spots," he said. "I don't mind going with you."

I soon found that he not only didn't mind, he was a rabid fisherman.

He climbed into the car, loaded with spinning gear.

"We'll try Cruz de Piedra Beach," he said. "It's 15 miles, so I hope you don't mind a little drive. A dusty one," he added. "But we might get some nice corvina."

Ten miles of the fifteen was on macadam road. Then we turned off into a desert road that meandered through cactus covered volcanic hills till I had completely lost all sense of direction. It was deep with sand and we left a cloud of dust to mark our course.

"Bet I could find my way out of here an hour from now, just by following that dust," I said.

We came to a Y in the road, and I stopped.

"Which way?"

"The right," yelled Hank. "Where the rag is tied on that branch as a marker. And keep moving! We'll smother!"

His warning came too late. Dust was pouring up through the floor boards, sifting in around the windows, as if the car were a sieve. I couldn't see to drive.

"Never stop on these roads unless you have to," Hank coughed, once we were under way, again. "There isn't a car made that will keep this dust out."

A road runner dashed across in front of us, his long legs really digging. A bit later a giant flycatcher soared up, snatched an insect and settled back on top of a cactus.

When we suddenly came through a little arroyo and I saw the blue waters of the Gulf of Lower California, I wanted to jump and run to it. I wanted to swim in it, loll in it, and wash away this layer of dust in it. But there was no time for that. We snatched our spinning rods and made for the beach.

"Try over there by the rocks," said Hank, indicating a spot on our left where the black, garbled looking rocks dropped down from a cliff and ran out into the water. The waves were breaking over them, throwing up a little spray. It looked like the place for fish, alright. A couple of crabs scuttled across at my feet, giving me further encouragement. With crabs around, there should be fish to feed on them.

I started out with a small white jig that had an upright hook so it didn't catch on the rocks. I made four or five casts without a hit, but down the beach I saw that Hank was into something. Gulls were working down that way, on a school of fish. A flight of pelicans went by, flying the prettiest formation I've ever seen. They went right over me and one of them set his wings, craned his head forward, lifted a leg and scratched his neck, then flapped a few times and caught up with his brethren.

The gulls were closer now, still working on that school of bait fish. I put on a big spoon and threw it out as far as I could. A fish hit it as soon as it landed and he must have been moving when he struck, because he couldn't possibly have gotten off to such a quick start from a standing position.

He fought like a mackerel, and that's what he was, a nice 5-pounder, a sierra. The school was almost to me, now, and things really picked up. I caught seven corbina and two more mackerel, one after the other, all about six pounds. This was a hot spot.

But suddenly everything went dead, the birds disappeared, and then Hank turned up beside me.

"Fishing's over, here," he said. "And I have to get back and look after my business. But we have time for a try at the hydro outlet."

"That's right in town," he explained. "It's where the water pours out of the generators at the power plant. There are often some nice fish in there."

We drove back to Guaymas, and to the downtown section right near the port. We crossed the railway tracks and pulled up where a pool was formed by the water pouring from a couple of huge pipes after it came from the turbines. It looked like a good trout pool, and there were currents and eddys and then the water went on out to the bay through a channel. Small fish were working in the channel as we stopped, and a couple of Mexican boys were dangling bait in the water.

Hank threw a weighted white feather up into the heavy current.

"What do you get here?" I asked.

"Pargo," he said. "Black pargo, red pargo."

He ended with a grunt as something socked his lure. The kids came running, and some workmen who had been repairing the railway crossing, put down their tools and came over.

That fish put a terrific bend in the rod.

"You'd better give him line," I told Hank. "He's going to break you up."

"This is no place to give line," he said. "And besides, this is 20 pound test."

He worked the fish in close, gave a mighty heave to his rod, and a brilliant red pargo came flying through the air. It dropped at his feet. The kids pounced on it and everyone yelled.

Hank retrieved his fish, took the hook out, and pushed the pargo back where it wouldn't flop into the water again. It looked like a good seven pounds.

He started to cast again, and so did I.

First thing I brought in was a flat, silver bodied fish.

"Pompano," said Hank. "You get everything here. That one is about three pounds."

Florence and Sy Margules fish the rocks near the Navy Yards at Guaymas.

It was different from *trachinotus carolinus*, the common pompano of the east. It didn't have the round, snub nose.

"It's the west coast pompano," said Hank.

I gave it to one of the little Mexican kids and he headed home with it, on the run. Hank landed another pargo and I rushed to get back into the act. I hooked one, and had it hot and heavy for ten minutes. He looked all of nine pounds. And then, just as I was about to land him, the hook pulled out.

The next cast I got a ladyfish and while I was releasing it, Hank brought in a six pound black pargo, a hard fighting fish. These Mexican snappers were real tough hombres.

"I'm afraid I have to go now," said Hank. "But you can see, can't you, that this is a good spot to fill in a little time."

I reckoned I was willing to fill in time like that any day! This was an extra dividend I hadn't expected on what had been planned to be a deep water charter boat fishing trip.

And all the dividends were not yet in. After lunch I met up with Ray Chapin of Long Beach, California, who had his trailer parked at the Miramar Hotel.

"I can show you a couple of spots," he volunteered. "If you don't mind a little drive. A dusty one," he went on. "But we might get a few corvina."

That speech had a familiar sound, but I said nothing. We drove ten miles on macadam road, then turned off on a desert road that meandered through cactus covered volcanic hills. A cloud of dust marked our path. But that time I knew better than to stop. When we came to the Y, Ray motioned to the right and I took the route marked with the rag tied on a branch like I'd never seen it before. In a few minutes we were on Cruz de Piedra Beach.

"Someone's been here already, today," said Ray, looking at the tracks Hank and I had left on the sand that morning.

I said nothing, except, "You think there are fish here?"

"Nearly always," said Ray. "Last year I took corvina up to 20 pounds right here. That was some of the best fishing I've ever had."

Later Ray was to prove it to me with pictures of those same fish but that day our best catch was a 5-pounder. But we had continuous action until we left.

"That's a good place, all right," I said as we drove away. "I've fished there all day and caught fish all day."

"You mean you were there this morning?" Ray asked. "Why didn't you tell me?"

"I was glad to come back," I said. "The fishing was better this afternoon than this morning. This beach has saved me from what I thought was going to be a two day blackout."

Ray told me that he'd been fishing the Guaymas area for 20 years.

"It's good light tackle fishing all year," he said. "with the best concentration of fish in the spring and summer months. There are pompano, ladyfish, red and black pargo, small roosterfish, jack crevalle, the corvina and the yellowfin corvina,

Corbina coming in. Along the rocks near the Navy Yard at Guaymas, Mexico.

the Spanish mackerel that we call sierra, flounders, called sole, that will hit deep, slow running bucktails, and some years ago a guy took a 24 pound permit."

Ray paused for breath, then went on. "Last year I took two five pound snook from shore," he said.

"How about further out?" I asked.

"All the fish you take from shore are there, too," he said. "And others like the skipjack, bonito and other fast moving school fish. There are more bait fish per square mile out there than any place I've ever been, so there are always lots of bigger fish feeding on them. And down underneath that, the bottom is paved with assorted fish, all plenty hungry if you can get your lure down to them."

Ray uses a small surf casting spin rod and I discovered that it was a lot more effective on beaches like Cruz de Piedro than was my smaller, regular spinning outfit because it would get the lure out a lot further. And as the beaches there shelf off too quickly for much deep wading, this was important.

"I've tried all lengths and weights of rods, down here," said Ray. "This one seems best. Most of the time we need to get far out and I can throw a big lure a long way with this rod. I can cast a smaller lure shorter distances, too, and with fair accuracy. With this outfit and a 10 pound test line I can handle almost any fish that comes along."

Ray uses yellow and white feathers, and weighted bucktails about four inches long, as well as half-ounce spoons. Almost any lure works well, including a big popping plug that got plenty of hits.

That evening Tom Jamison called me.

"You've got one more day to fill in," he said. "Come over here to my office and meet Bill Groves. He'll take you somewhere tomorrow."

Bill is an American who lives in Guaymas and knows the area pretty thoroughly. I told him I had already been to Cruz de Piedro, and to the outlet of the electric plant.

"Then we should try the Empalme bridge tomorrow," he

said. "You may have to dodge a few trains and cars, but it's good fishing."

Empalme is a small town immediately adjacent to Guaymas and a combined highway and train bridge leads to it across an inlet from the bay. The car right of way is a single lane and it seemed to me that most of the drivers, American and Mexican alike, raced each other from opposite directions, to see who could get on it first. We figured it was safer to walk out along the railway trestle and fish from there.

The tide was running out hard beneath us and several Mexicans who were fishing with handlines already had fish, one a nice eight pound corvina.

We would cast into the current that flowed under the bridge like a river, let the lure drift across until it was straight below us, and then retrieve. Half an hour later we had half a dozen corvina, the largest a nine pounder.

Just as we were getting ready to leave, a train whistled and came chugging across the trestle, scattering everyone out on ledges and rocks until it had passed. But no sooner had the caboose clippety-clopped onto land again than they were all back there fishing.

"We'll have to hurry now," said Bill. "I want to hit San Pedro Beach on the right tide."

We missed the tide at San Pedro but we did get in on the making of some angling history. On our way over to the beach we stopped at Miramar and picked up Cy Margules and his wife Florence, of Roslyn Heights, Long Island, N. Y. Cy had never done any spinning and wanted to learn how, so I fitted him up with an enclosed American type reel, a Johnson Century, and sent him along the beach to practice. He soon caught on to the casting and kept working away at it while we chased up and down after a school of slashing, hard feeding yellowfin corvina that never did hit our lures.

Then we heard a yell and saw that Cy had a fish on. It wasn't big but was giving him a pretty good fight, and we all moved down to watch him beach it,

"My first fish on spinning tackle!" he said proudly.

"Be careful!" I yelled. I grabbed his fish and carried it well back from the water's edge. "Allow me to be the first to congratulate you. You have probably landed the first bonefish ever taken here on an artificial lure."

"You've just made angling history," Bill Groves agreed. "There are lots of bonefish here. A couple of anglers caught 200 in one day not long ago, using small hooks and small pieces of bait. But everyone has always said that they wouldn't hit artificials."

Cy beamed. Then he looked at the size of the fish.

"It's mighty small," he said. "Wish it could have been bigger."

"With that light tackle, a two pound bonefish gives a nice fight," I said. "And besides, he's about par for the bonefish out here. According to the experts they seldom go above 2½ pounds here."

By then the tide was far out, so Bill suggested moving on to another of his "hot spots." This time it was the steep, rocky shore along the bay near, the Navy Yard.

It took a mountain goat to navigate those big, sharp-edged, loose rocks from the road down to the comparatively safe footing along the shore, but we made it. A local angler was there ahead of us, and he was having a rough time of it. He was a young fellow, dressed in his Sunday suit, and he told us in very broken English that he was down from Hermosillo for the day, hoping to take home some fish to justify the trip.

"My poppa will not like if I catch not fish," he said seriously.

As he cast, I made a mental bet with myself that it was a sure thing that Poppa was in for "not like." The boy had what looked like the first plug rod and trolling reel ever made, all neatly fitted out with line that must have gone at least 90 pound test. On the end of it he had tied a gigantic silver spoon. With that lure, if he caught anything, it had to be big!

He would get up on his toes, go away back with his arms, and then come forward with a heave that should have thrown

Well-known west coast photographer, Ray Chapin of Long Beach, California, wades out in Cruz de Piedra Bay, casting for big yellowfin corbina.

the spoon all the way across the bay into the main street of Guaymas. But something was wrong with his timing. With a mighty swoosh, every time, the lure would plunge into the water practically at his feet. Once he got out 15 feet, but that was his best effort.

This was killing me, but I figured I was there to fish, not to teach. I made a cast and caught a 2-pound corvina. I saw his face as I reeled it in, and I felt like a heel.

"Would you like to have this fish?" I asked.

His face lighted up. He grabbed that corvina and stuffed it into a big cardboard box with which he had optimistically came prepared. Then he started heaving that spoon again.

I cast and caught another.

"Here's an extra dividend," I said, throwing it to him.

Grinning wider than ever, he put that one in the box. Then Bill Groves caught one and it was added to the pile. This went on until the box was nearly full, and each time we handed

him a fish, we'd say, "Here's a little extra dividend for you."
We felt meaner all the time, catching so many while he caught
none.

At last, as we kept on catching them, and he kept on casting and never getting out far enough to even reel in, his bright-
ness began to fade. I couldn't stand it any more. I called him
over and handed him my rod and reel.

"Let's see you cast this,", I suggested. "But not so hard."

Having seen the force he put behind the heavy outfit, I
figured that with a decent one he'd probably hit Tom Jamison
on the head, somewhere out there in the Gulf of Lower
California.

"Easy!" I urged, unloosing the death grip he had taken on
the rod handle.

He didn't understand many of the words, but he caught
the meaning. He flipped the rod gently, out went the lure,
and before he had time to think he had a strike.

He didn't catch that first one because he acted as if he still
had that 90 pound test line. He horsed the fish and broke it
off. But on his second cast he hooked another, and with much
coaching from the sidelines, finally reeled it in. It wasn't a big
one, only about a pound and a half, but to him it was more
precious than all the others in the box.

"I go now," he said. "But I return in one minute."

He scrambled up over the rocks, put the box down beside
his car, then came all the way back down and shook our hands.

"Senors," he said. "Those good dividends! I cannot return
them like you. But I wish for you, somehow, some day—
maybe not in this world, but in the next—si—I wish you many
dividends."

We all grinned sheepishly at each other. But we were all
thinking the same thing. What better dividend could a guy
ask, than good fishing in the next world?

17. Trout In The Sky

Having gone as far as we could, laterally, in Montana, we decided to try "up."

IT WAS SIX A.M. and we were sitting in a restaurant at Silver Gate, Montana, 7000 feet high on the Red Lodge Pass. A moose and her calf were ambling down the main street. Our pack string was tied across the road at Elmer Larson's Switchback Lodge, and in the still morning air we could hear the horses restlessly stamping their feet, occasionally neighing. Moose and calf paid no attention, wandered on and disappeared behind a log cabin.

From across the road, Johnny Linderman signalled us that he was ready to go.

There were just the three outfitters, Elmer Larsen, Gene Wade, and Johnny Linderman, and five of us dudes—Grace and Walt Weber, Bill Browning, and myself and wife. Walt was after pictures and sketches of alpine wildlife; Bill was after pictures, and I was just there for the fishing, to get some of those big brookies that were rumored to reside in well named Aero Lake.

"Elmer and I have seen them in there up to five pounds," said Gene. "The best looking fish I've ever caught, fat and bright and full of pep."

"I've never been in to Aero Lake before," said Johnny. "But I have been over it. I helped stock it from an airplane, back in 1937. I've been as far as timberline on horseback, since, but never up those last 2000 feet."

"But this string can make it," he added.

We looked at the horses with a mixture of dread and confidence. We knew that a Linderman, member of one of America's best known cowboy families, would produce a good string of horses. What we didn't know was our own ability to stay on a good horse on such a ride as we were about to start.

It was a lung-busting climb. Aero Lake lies 11,500 feet high in the remote Upper Beartooth Range of Southern Montana. Twenty-five miles south as the crow flies, we could often spot Pilot and Index Peaks, famous landmarks for every traveller through this Montana-Wyoming border country. And about the same distance to our north the Grasshopper Glacier put a nip in the wind that could still be felt even at this distance. Close to Grasshopper was Granite Peak, the highest point in Montana, rising 12,850 feet into the sky.

The first part of the ride was through foothill country, if it can be called foothill when you are working up from 7000 to 8000 feet. But that was what the horses apparently considered it, and an old wagon road provided a good trail, so we ambled right along. But at 9000 feet the trail petered out into a narrow path through lodge pole pine. Almost at the same minute the temperature seemed to drop. We put on leather jackets over wool sweaters, donned gloves, and then really began to climb. We worked up through the timber on switchback trails, crossing sudden glades where there were deer and elk sign, and spooky clumps of pine where the horses shied at the scent of bear. Then suddenly we were out above the timber line and riding through shale and jagged rock that kept both horse and rider tense. It was practically straight up climbing, with the horses digging in with all fours and the riders hanging on the same way. We found out what saddle horns were for.

At last we came to what looked like a perpendicular wall,

Fat brook trout from Aero Lake, near Cooke City, Montana.

only a few chipped rocks showing where at some time a horse had gone up there, scrambling and plunging.

"Get a good grip and hang on," said Elmer. "This is pretty steep."

That was the understatement of the day. Even though the climb was short to the ledge we could see above us, it was the longest, hardest part of the trip. The grade was so steep that a horse could only make a couple of plunging steps before he had to stop to breathe and brace himself for the next lunge. Every movement sent sparks flying as iron clad hooves scraped the rock. Only the fact that I had heard about the law of gravity convinced me that we were not actually climbing on an outward incline.

But at last, one by one, our horses scrambled over the top, and onto a narrow ledge which ran along the side of the mountain. We dismounted and threw ourselves down to rest, as winded from that rocky ride as if we had climbed every step of the way on foot.

Above us rose a gigantic mass of rock, forming a jagged skyline.

"The lake lies behind that," said Gene.

"We're on foot from here," said John Linderman. "Horses can't get over that divide."

He spoke with the heartfelt sadness of the cowboy who has no use for walking. And as we looked up to the divide, we shared his sadness. From here there was not even a hint of a path, only great, rounded boulders that must have been piled there by some ancient glacier. It might be duck soup to a mountain goat, but it was no place for a tenderfoot.

"John will take the horses back down to pasture," said Elmer. "The rest of us will each pack what we can over the divide."

"Take a light load," instructed Gene. "Don't forget, you're at 11,000 feet right now, and carrying will be tough."

Gene and Elmer each heaved a deflated rubber boat on their shoulders while the rest of us picked up loads from the welter of sleeping bags, air mattresses cooking gear and fishing tackle that Johnny was unloading from the pack horses.

Elmer looked at what we had chosen and grinned.

"Take about half that much," he advised.

Then he and Gene started away, climbing slowly but steadily. We followed but within seconds were puffing and blowing, discarding part of our loads and finally collapsing on the boulders every two minutes to get our wind again. Elmer and Gene passed us on their way back for a second load before we had even reached the summit. They were beside us again with their second pack when we came over the top.

"Right pretty, isn't it?" said Elmer, as we stood spellbound.

Before us lay Aero Lake, a glittering gem of blue set in the midst of one of the bleakest Arctic scenes I have ever seen. The lake was almost circular, with two long arms running off into the distance and two little islands half way across. They had told us we would camp on the far island, and now we saw why. The mainland on which we stood was a solid mass of boulders, similar to the pass which we had just traversed. There was not a single square foot of land anywhere in which to sink a tent peg, just rocks, rocks, some as big as houses. Here and there the remains of a glacier running down to the shore afforded the easiest means of approach to the lake. All around us jagged peaks rose to poke at the sky, all bare and brown, without any vegetation at all, while lower down on our own level were only a few dwarfed bushes. It was as desolate as tundra country, bleak and forbidding, but lovely.

We stepped out onto the nearest snow field, following Elmer's and Gene's tracks toward the shore.

Suddenly Walt stopped and pointed down. I looked.

"Hey, Elmer!" I yelled. "What's this? The snow is bleeding!"

Elmer came back to see what we meant.

Everywhere he and Gene had stepped, the snow glowed red in their foot prints.

"Insects," he said. "Thousands of tiny insects that live in the snow and only show up when you step where they are."

"They certainly must be small," I said.

"Look at those stunted cedars and willows," he replied. "And the only animals you'll see are the cony and a small ground squirrel. Everything is undersize up here."

"Everything but the fish," he added. "You don't need to worry about them being undersized."

In the lake, which lay 25 feet below us, the water was so clear that you could have seen a penny on the bottom. The rocks shelved out quickly to a drop-off with here and there wide ledges running out just under the surface, ideal hiding spots for trout.

"You go ahead and fish," said Elmer. "We'll set up camp on the island and then pick you up wherever you are along the shore."

Walt started around the lake to the right, while I went to the left. It was rough going, a constant scramble over boulders,

Horses are packed and ready to go. From here on it will be mountain trail.

and once I had to circle a 200 foot snow bank which dropped off sheer into the water like the edge of a glacier. I was afraid to try to cross it for fear it would crumble away beneath me and I would be plunged into water so icy that a man couldn't last in it for five minutes.

The fishing was rough, too, and though I tried streamers, bucktails, nymphs, wet flies and dry flies, I didn't raise the first fish. By late afternoon I was better than a mile away from the pass, on the far shore of the lake. And there, at last, in a long, narrow bay marking the inlet of a small stream that splashed down from Upper Aero Lake, still higher above us, I found the fish.

I was working my way over the high cliff along the inlet when I looked down and there they were, several good sized trout feeding along the drop-off, turning as they fed, so that their bodies flashed silver and red.

I was too high above them to fish from the cliff but further along I spotted a four foot wide ledge just three feet above the water, and somehow I scrambled down to that.

I dropped a black ant near those fish and it hadn't sunk three inches before there was a flash and line and leader jumped forward. I lifted the rod tip and watched it bend down as that husky trout hit and headed out. When he stopped, he began to wag his head from side to side and I couldn't budge him with the light leader I was using. I just stood there, holding my own and watching the beautiful red glow that shone all around him in the water.

"He's a big one," I thought. "And a beautiful one. He gives out like a Christmas tree light."

He kept rocking the rod for a while, then switched back down the inlet and scared me when it appeared that he would go under a rock and cut me off. Then he headed out again, and pretty soon I had him coming my way. When I finally did land him, he was the deepest, fattest, prettiest Eastern Brook trout I have ever seen, a bit over two pounds.

A few minutes later I had two more just like him and an almost equally beautiful pair of cutthroats that went about two and one-half pounds apiece. Their sides were crimson, and their bellies too, with a liberal sprinkling of big black spots, light towards the front, and heavy towards the tail.

Just as I got my knife out to clean the fish Walt came up behind me.

"I didn't raise a thing around the other shore," he said. "I tried everything in the book, too. I even dug around in the water to see what they might be feeding on, but couldn't find a thing."

Then he saw the fish.

"Where'd you get them?" he asked.

"Right here," I answered.

Walt grabbed the knife out of my hand.

"Let me clean them," he said. "I want to see what's in them."

He kneeled at the water's edge and slit up the belly of a

brookie and laid the flesh back. It was deep red, darker than salmon.

"Did you ever see such beautiful messenaries?" said Walt with awe in his voice.

I looked around hurriedly. Nothing unusual appeared near us or on the horizon.

"Where?" I asked. "What?"

"The messenaries," said Walt, ever the scientist, pointing with his knife tip. "Those magenta colored sacs, there."

He meant the cellophane-like case which contained the guts of the fish.

"The fish with the beautiful guts," I grinned. "First time I ever heard anyone call a fish's guts beautiful."

Walt, meantime, had slit the stomach sac and now he came up with a mess of black, spotted here and there with what looked like bits of red pepper. He held the mass in his cupped hands and put them into the water. The mass separated into small pieces, some black, some red.

"It's like Elmer told us," Walt said. "Everything is on the small scale up here. Those are daphnia—water fleas. The red ones are some kind of tiny fresh water shrimp that I've never seen before. I'll send a few in to the lab and find out what they are."

Next he pried open the mouth of the fish and we both peered in. A sprinkling of small black dots adhered to the roof, and a few showed in the gills.

"That must be the way they feed," said Walt. "They get into a school of those little fleas and swim through with their mouths open. They're too small to take individually."

He took out his pocket handkerchief and wrapped the wet mass of fleas and shrimp he had collected, and stuck it in his pocket.

"Well, let's go feed them something larger," I suggested, and we both grabbed our rods and started off.

But though we fished for another half hour, we didn't find any more fish. Then Gene showed up in one of the rubber

The author casting at the arm of the inlet, as others in the party are ferried back to the island camp in the undamaged boat.

boats and we started back to the island, picking Bill up en route, from further along the shore.

"I've got two in the ice box," he said, pointing to the snow bank behind him.

There in the gleaming snow he had carved out the words HIGH LAKE TROUT, and close by lay two nice trout, a native and a brookie.

We had fish for dinner and besides being the most beautiful fish we had ever seen, they were the best eating.

The next day was a terrible let down. We fished the whole morning without a strike. We fished from boats and from shore. We went out to the reefs that showed here and there beneath the clear water. But not the first strike and never a sign of a fish. Gene and Elmer were shaking their heads gloomily.

"There's weather coming," suggested Elmer. "That will put high altitude fish down."

But the sky was clear and bright, the lake placid. And there were no fish.

By three o'clock we were all spread along the arm of the cove where I had taken those few trout on the previous afternoon. The two rubber boats were pulled up on the shore, one in the cove, the other at the mouth of the cove. We were all fishing from shore, trying, but our hearts were not in it.

And suddenly Elmer's weather prophecy came all too true. We heard a far off, rushing sound, and instantaneously the lake began to build up waves, big ones, like breakers on the sea. Before we could get back to the boats a blast of wind roared down on us, loaded with the chill of the Grasshopper Glacier, 25 miles to the north. It created havoc.

Grace Weber was only a few feet from the edge of the cliff on one side of the cove. I saw her sway in the wind and grabbed her just in time. Hanging on to each other, we managed to withstand the buffeting of that mighty blast. Across the cove we saw Mary throw herself down on the ground for safety. Then everyone was looking up.

A big yellow boat was soaring over our heads, fifty feet high, closely followed by a cowboy hat. It was seconds before it dawned on us that it was one of our lifeboats. Everyone started to run, forgetting wind, forgetting altitude and rough terrain.

We staggered over the rim of a little dip in time to see the lifeboat crash to the ground and grind into tatters on three big jagged rocks. The cowboy hat floated down beside it, in the now dying wind.

Bill Browning came puffing up.

"My hat," he said inanely, picking it up and jamming it on his head. "I tried to hold it—the boat, I mean. But I couldn't. The wind lifted it right out of the water and carried it away."

"The other boat!" Gene and Elmer both yelled at once.

We all had the same thought. If the other boat was done for, too, we were stranded here, in bleak, forbidding country, without food or extra clothing. All our supplies were on the island, with half a mile of ice cold water between.

Just then we spotted the second boat, floating down the inlet towards us, one oar still in it, the other floating a few yards away. The onshore wind was driving it towards us. We all rushed down to meet it.

It, too, had several bad gashes, but at least it was still afloat. Elmer looked it over carefully.

"That just about fixes our trip," he said. "We have eight people, we're camped on an island, and we have one badly damaged five man boat. We'll have to try to patch it and start ferrying back to the island, two or three at a time. We'll break camp first thing in the morning and ferry over to the pass the same way. It means cutting the trip two days short, but there's no other way to do it. You can't take risks in this kind of country."

He started to work on the boat, then took a look at our glum faces.

"You might as well fish while you can," he said. "I'll take the women back to camp first, then pick you up on the second trip."

We didn't need any further invitation.

"I have an idea that storm may have wakened the fish up," said Walt.

And how right he was. Fish were everywhere. We had hits right and left. We caught them spinning and fly fishing, on streamers, ants, nymphs, spoons and jig type lures. They liked everything. We caught plenty of 2-pounders, a few 3-pounders, and a couple of 4-pounders. We kept six for dinner and threw the rest back with the admonition to grow even bigger. They were still hitting hard when Elmer came back for us to take us to camp.

"I shouldn't take the time," he said. "That boat is in pretty tough shape and I want to get us out of here. But I just have to catch me one of those beauties."

He grabbed Bill's rod and made a cast and in minutes had

landed as bright and beautiful a brookie as I've ever seen.

"One more," he said. "One for the road. Let me try one on a fly, Joe."

I gave him my outfit, and he made a couple of nice casts. Suddenly the big one we'd all been hoping for socked that fly. We all saw him flash up and hit, illuminating the water around him with his brilliant color. He busted that leader point like it had been a cobweb. He was a good 6 pounds.

"Well," said Elmer, trying to look unconcerned. "I knew there were some big ones in here."

"It'll give me something to come back for," he said, quite a few minutes later, as he rowed us back to the island.

And we all agreed, "Me, too."

Sportsman's Vintage Press
Available at www.SportsmansVintagePress.com

All books are available to order as hard copy and some books are available as a free PDF download. Visit **www.SportsmansVintagePress.com** for a full description and chapter listing of each title and follow us on Twitter **@SVPress** for updates on sales and new releases.